Little Red Book
of
Word Power

By the same author

Little Red Book Series

- Little Red Book of Slang-Chat Room Slang
- Little Red Book of English Vocabulary Today
- Little Red Book of Grammar Made Easy
- Little Red Book of English Proverbs
- Little Red Book of Prepositions
- Little Red Book of Idioms and Phrases
- Little Red Book of Euphemisms
- Little Red Book of Effective Speaking Skills
- Little Red Book of Modern Writing Skills
- Little Red Book of Verbal Phrases
- Little Red Book of Synonyms
- Little Red Book of Antonyms
- Little Red Book of Common Errors
- Little Red Book of Letter Writing
- Little Red Book of Perfect Written English
- Little Red Book of Essay Writing
- Little Red Book of Word Fact
- Little Red Book of Spelling
- Little Red Book of Language Checklist

A2Z Book Series

- A2Z Quiz Book
- A2Z Book of Word Origins

Others

- The Book of Fun Facts
- The Book of More Fun Facts
- The Book of Firsts and Lasts
- The Book of Virtues
- The Book of Motivation
- Read Write Right: Common Errors in English
- The Students' Companion

Little Red Book *of* Word Power

Terry O'Brien

RUPA

Published by
Rupa Publications India Pvt. Ltd 2012
7/16, Ansari Road, Daryaganj
New Delhi 110002

Sales centres:
Allahabad Bengaluru Chennai
Hyderabad Jaipur Kathmandu
Kolkata Mumbai

Copyright © Terry O'Brien 2012

All rights reserved.
No part of this publication may be reproduced, transmitted, or stored in a retrieval system, in any form or by any means, electronic, mechanical, photocopying, recording or otherwise, without the prior permission of the publisher.

ISBN: 978-81-291-2107-3

Ninth impression 2022

15 14 13 12 11 10 9

The moral right of the author has been asserted.

Typeset by Innovative Processors, New Delhi

Printed in India

This book is sold subject to the condition that it shall not, by way of trade or otherwise, be lent, resold, hired out, or otherwise circulated, without the publisher's prior consent, in any form of binding or cover other than that in which it is published.

*I dedicate this book to late Prof. A.P. O'Brien,
my father, friend, guide and mentor, who
inspired me to the canon of excellence:
re-imagining what's essential*

PREFACE

Some people think learning more and more words can strengthen us in our communication. But beware, it is time to understand the subtle difference in the use of some words. **Little Red Book of Word Power** is not a run-on-the-mill book of word power. It aims at the approach to learn words as a pleasurable activity. Words move; music moves!

Avoid the hit-and-run method of learning words by rote. **Little Red Book of Word Power** is a book to help you understand the limits and extent of words, be it a simple or a complex word. The approach is one to have fun while finding the thin lines between words that seem the same yet are so different. The bottom line is loud and clear: I'd rather be right!

A

ABUSE or MISUSE

Abuse is a more serious term, constantly appearing in phrases like child abuse. **To abuse** means to 'make bad use of'. As noun or verb it can describe the physical (usually sexual), verbal or psychological mistreatment of others. When applied to drink and drugs, the word suggests an excessive, uncontrolled intake of the substance in question.

To **misuse** is to 'use for the wrong purpose'.

ACCEPT or EXCEPT

To **accept** is to 'receive':

✓ I accepted her kind offer of help.

The less common verb to **except** means to 'take out', to 'exclude':

✓ He was excepted from the criticism which the rest of the committee earned. (**Except** is also a preposition meaning 'not including'.)

ACETIC or ASCETIC

Two words quite easily confused in their spelling. And, perhaps at some subconscious level, the vinegary sense of one suggests the self-punishing sense of the other!

Acetic defines an acid which in a diluted form is vinegar:

✓ You can sweeten onions even more by rinsing them in vinegar: the acetic acid in it will mask the remaining sulphur compounds.

The adjective **ascetic** means 'denying oneself bodily pleasure for moral or religious reasons'. Somebody who lives like this full-time is an ascetic.

✓ So you cut out coffee, cigarettes, carbohydrates, dairy products, red meat — anything to keep up the ascetic high.

ACQUIESCE, ASSENT or AGREE

These three words occupy the same sort of area but have different shades of meaning.

To **acquiesce** is to 'consent without showing opposition':

✓ He acquiesced in the plans although he had no part in making them.

To **assent** has a slightly formal tone to it and means to 'comply', to 'agree to' (usually without much eagerness). Agree covers these two senses but also extends to more positive meanings: to 'be of one mind with', 'be compatible with'.

ACTIVE or PROACTIVE

The choice between this pair of closely connected words has more to do with fashion than meaning.

✓ There's something about **proactive** which sets my teeth on edge.

A few years ago **proactive** was a buzzword, an unwelcome newcomer on the fringes, but it has made the transition into ordinary English, or at least as ordinary as the English you find in official lingo.

Not as a synonym for 'very active', which is sometimes how it's used (with the underlying thought of **'You may be**

active but I'm proactive'), but in the sense of 'instigating change' or 'acting without being prompted'. The word is really the counterpart of 'reactive'.

ACTOR or ACTRESS

One of a group of word-pairs describing professions where the neutral form has traditionally been reserved for the male sex. The problem comes with the 'feminine' form of each pair.

The tendency is to avoid words that designate the sex of the person carrying out a particular job, thus 'firefighter' is preferred to 'fireman'. An **actor** describes a person who acts on stage, film or TV irrespective of sex.

> (The difference between 'actor' and 'star' would make for an interesting and subtle difference — not all actors have star quality but most stars refer to themselves as actors when they want to be taken seriously.)

Other art forms are also home to unisex terms like 'author', 'poet', 'sculptor'. There are feminine forms of some of these terms: **'authoress', 'poetess'**. Now they sound out of date. Even in ballet, the feminine 'ballerina' has generally been replaced by 'dancer'. The feminine form may sometimes be retained — waiter/waitress; steward/stewardess; headmaster/headmistress — although, as far as the last two are concerned, there is a preference now for the sexually unrevealing 'flight attendant', and 'principal' for the head of a school. Job advertisements, wary of accusations of discrimination now refer to hybrid beings called 'waitpersons' or 'post persons'. One of the fields where the sex difference still holds is the host/hostess distinction. 'Hostess' leads a kind of double life: ultra-respectable at a dinner party but slightly sleazy in a nightclub. 'Host' can be used for either sex.

AD HOC or AD LIB

Both of these Latin expressions are concerned with things done at short notice, and are sometimes treated as though they are interchangeable. They're not.

Ad hoc means '(organised) for a particular purpose rather than being permanent. Ad hoc arrangements tend to be makeshift:

✓ He is an ad hoc teacher.

Ad lib (from ad libitum — 'at will') means 'spontaneous', 'unrehearsed'. It generally applies to off-the-cuff speakers, who will get a reputation for ad-libbing if they make a habit of it:

✓ On stage, he was an ad lib humorist.

ADOPTED or ADOPTIVE

Adopted applies to the person who is being adopted (or to the plan, suggestion, etc.)

✓ The adopted children were likely to go through great trouble.

Adoptive describes those who are doing the adopting – this word can only be applied to those adopting children, not to the children themselves.

ADVERSE or AVERSE

Two adjectives with a one-letter difference; they both carry a general sense of 'against'.

The adjective **adverse** means opposing or 'unfavourable.'

✓ Adverse weather conditions delayed our journey.

Averse is very often coupled with 'not' - as in

✓ 'I'm not averse to your suggestion'.

Such a sentence suggests a willingness to be persuaded rather than enthusiasm about something, and so carries a valuable shade of meaning.

Averse means 'reluctant', 'unwilling'.

ADVICE or ADVISE

The spelling differs by one letter between the noun and verb forms. When it comes to **advice/advise,** mistakes like the following are quite usual:

…you will be introduced to your boss who will give you all the advise [should be advice] you need. . .

Advice is the noun form and the one which should have been used in the example above, while **advise** is the verb:

✓ We received some good advice [noun]/He advised us well [verb] (But the person giving the advice is an adviser.)

AFFECT or EFFECT

Two words that sound very similar and which are frequently mixed up. To add to the confusion, the noun which relates to the main meaning of affect is effect.

As a verb **affect** means to 'have an impact on', 'make a difference to':

✓ Rohit's drinking affected his health more than his personality.

Also, as a verb *affect* has the less usual meaning of 'to put on', to 'pretend'.

To **effect** is to 'bring about', to 'carry through':

✓ They effected most changes almost overnight.

The noun which relates to the verb **affect** and has the same general sense of 'impact' is not, as one might expect, affect but **effect**:

✓ The harmful effects of cigarette smoking are now well established.

AFFLICT or INFLICT

These are two similar-sounding words, both suggesting suffering and punishment.

If a condition **afflicts** a person or animal it causes them 'trouble' or 'distress':

✓ Delhi Belly (diarrhoea) is a more widespread problem, afflicting at least two-fifths of all international travellers.

To **inflict** is to 'impose something unpleasant on someone'. This word focuses more on the punishment, condition, etc.

AGGRAVATE and ANNOY

The primary meaning of **aggravate** is to 'make worse'.

By contrast, **annoy** often means no more than 'irritate':

✓ She was annoyed by the frequent interruptions to her work.

ALIBI or EXCUSE

An **alibi**, more precise and forceful than an excuse, is a defence (often in court) that denotes one was 'elsewhere at the time' (this is its literal meaning from Latin).

An excuse is sometimes just an 'explanation':
✓ Her excuse for being late was that her alarm clock hadn't gone off.

ALLEVIATE or AMELIORATE

To **alleviate** is to 'make lighter'. It's generally applied to moods, emotional burdens, pain, or states of mind.

To **ameliorate** is to 'bring about an improvement'. The tendency is to use the word about physical conditions (illness, poverty, etc.).

ALLOT, A LOT or ALOT

Allot means to 'parcel out' (the noun is allotment). It has nothing to do with **a lot** (i.e. a 'large quantity'). But the real error comes when these last two words are written as one — 'alot'. **Alot** is always wrong.

ALL RIGHT or ALRIGHT

Probably under the influence of words such as 'already' and 'altogether', there is a growing tendency to run together the two parts of all right.

Alright is especially common in informal contexts — 'It'll be alright at night' — but is regarded by what is probably a diminishing number as less correct than **all right**. Even so it is better avoided in formal writing.

ALLUSION, ILLUSION or DELUSION

Allusion has a meaning distinct from that of the other two. An allusion is an 'indirect reference' and it's often found in discussion of music, films, and so on (where it indicates references to other bits of music, verse, etc.).

Illusion and **delusion** are both to do with a 'mistaken idea' or a 'false belief'.

A **delusion,** however, is not something that is easily driven away by argument or brutal fact, as it may be a sign of madness:

✓ He began to suffer from the delusion that he was the final authority.

ALTAR or ALTER

The **altar** (noun only) is the 'communion table' in church or a 'place for making sacrifices'. **Alter** (verb only) means to 'change' (noun: alteration).

ALTERNATE or ALTERNATIVE

There's a clear distinction between these two, but they both contain the ideas of 'otherness' and 'change' and are frequently confused.

Alternative can be used as a noun or adjective, and indicates that another thing is being offered.

Alternate is both adjective and verb. As an adjective, it means occurring by turns 'every other':

✓ We have holidays on alternate Saturdays.

As a verb, **alternate** means to 'shift from one thing to another and then back again':

✓ Her moods alternated between euphoria and gloom.

The adjectival form of alternate shouldn't be used as a substitute for alternative:

✗ The city was an alternate [should be alternative] target and was bombed two days earlier than planned.

(This suggests that the city was bombed by turns with another target.)

Alternative also describes technology medicine, comedy, etc. which is not mainstream.

ALTOGETHER or ALL TOGETHER

Like a number of words and phrases involving the prefix 'al-' and the complete word 'all' — 'already/all ready', 'alright/all right' — these are sometimes confused, particularly because the two words run into one when spoken aloud.

Altogether (an adverb) means 'entirely', 'with everything included':

✓ The birthday girl was altogether delighted with her presents.

✓ The newly married couple made seven trips during the year altogether.

All together means occurring 'simultaneously' or 'in the same place'.

AMBIGUOUS or AMBIVALENT

Ambiguous is an adjective meaning 'unclear', 'of doubtful meaning'.

Being **ambivalent** involves a more thought-out position since it means 'being in two minds' or 'experiencing conflicting emotions about something'.

   (The noun forms are ambiguity and ambivalence.)

AMEND or EMEND

To **amend** is to 'improve by changing or correcting.'

To **emend** has the more restricted sense of 'make alterations in a written text.'

AMIABLE or AMICABLE

Amiable means 'friendly', 'likeable':

✓ He was popular for his easy-going and amiable manner.

Amicable means 'in a friendly spirit', and tends to be found in situations where differences of opinion have been resolved without a quarrel, or where bad relations might be expected:

✓ They divorced a year later and all seemed amicable.

AMNESTY or MORATORIUM

An **amnesty** is a 'general pardon' or describes a 'period in which crimes can be admitted to without penalty':

✓ The President has the power of amnesty.

A **moratorium** describes a 'stretch of time when an activity is halted'. It is often applied to the suspension of debt payment but has wider uses.

AMONG, AMONGST or BETWEEN

There's no difference between **among** and **amongst,** although the first version of the word is more widely used. There's no great difference between **among** and **between**.

AMORAL or IMMORAL

Amoral means 'outside accepted systems of morality'. The word implies lack of the conception of right and wrong. Animals are amoral, for example.

Immoral means 'contrary to accepted standards of morality'. The word frequently has a sexual application.

ANNEX or ANNEXE

There's a difference between the noun and verb forms of this word, and it is easy to confuse the two.

To **annex** (pronounced with a stress on the second syllable) is to 'attach', 'take possession of'.

An **annexe** (with a final 'e' and pronounced with the stress more on the first syllable) is an 'extension', a 'building attached to a larger one.'

ANOINT or APPOINT

To **anoint** was originally to 'smear with oil as an act of consecration'.

To **appoint** is simply to 'select for a position':
✓ She was appointed managing director at a relatively early age.

ANTICIPATE or EXPECT

These two verbs are widely treated as if they were interchangeable but there is a useful difference in meaning between them.

To **anticipate** is not merely to believe that something will happen (i.e. expect), but to 'take some action to prevent or lessen the consequences of what will occur'. Where expect is largely passive:

✓ They're expecting it to rain tomorrow.

Anticipate- has more active overtones:

✓ Anticipating rain, she took her umbrella with her.

ANXIETY or ANGST

Although **anxiety** has a special medical application (describing an aspect of depression) the general sense of the word is 'worry', a 'nagging concern.'

Angst (from the German) also means 'anxiety', but it has philosophical overtones suggesting troubled soul-searching. Angst is anxiety with attitude.

APOLOGIA or APOLOGY

Despite the look of the first word, it has almost nothing to do with saying sorry or expressing regret.

An **apologia** (pronounced with the stress on the long second 'o') is a 'formal statement in the defence or justification of a particular position'.

An **apology** is an 'expression of sorrow or regret', sometimes on others behalf but usually for oneself.

APPRAISE or APPRISE

The verb **appraise** means to 'sum up', to 'estimate the value or quality of' something or somebody.

> (The noun is **appraisal** - a pseudo-technical-sounding word now most often applied to the way in which employees are assessed by their bosses.)

To **apprise** (slightly formal rather than in everyday use) is to 'give notice to', 'tell'.

ARBITER, ARBITRATOR or MEDIATOR

These three terms, all describing people who assess situations and sort out problems, are sometimes used interchangeably but they have distinct shades of meaning.

An **arbiter** is an 'umpire', one who lays down the law or sets a standard of taste.

An **arbitrator** is 'someone brought in to settle a dispute'. This word, rather than arbiter, tends to be used in trade disputes and the law.

A **mediator** is an 'individual who acts as a go-between', sometimes when two or more parties are in disagreement, but often simply to keep things running smoothly.

ARCHETYPE or STEREOTYPE

An **archetype** is the 'original model from which copies are produced'.

A **stereotype** is a 'clichéd image', 'something which conforms completely to a standard pattern', and there is usually a negative shading to the word.

ARDENT or ARDUOUS

Ardent means 'burning with enthusiasm'.

Arduous means 'difficult to achieve' or 'tough'.

AROMA or ODOUR

Two nouns meaning 'smell': But is one more positive than the other?

If there's a difference it is that **aroma** tends to be applied to pleasant scents, particularly from food or drinks:

✓ I can still recall the delicious aroma of teas from around the world.

Odour is more neutral and wide-ranging. In fact it's generally associated with the less attractive smells such as body odour.

AROUSE or ROUSE

To **arouse** is to 'excite', to 'provoke', and is usually applied to reactions (interest, concern) or feelings (suspicion, anger).

Arouse is also used for sexual responses, as is the associated noun, arousal.

To **rouse** is to 'awaken', to 'stir up' and generally takes a person or animal as its object:

✓ The temple bells roused him from his sleep.

AS IF or LIKE

The use of **like** as a link-word (conjunction) instead of as if or as though is very frequent:

✓ She looked like she had some good news to tell (rather than the more correct…as if she had…).

ASSUMPTION or PRESUMPTION

An **assumption** can be a 'supposition which isn't supported by evidence'; 'false' is the adjective often partnered with it and, even if it turns out to be correct, it has more the sense of a 'guess'.

A **presumption** has more the sense of a 'probability', i.e. it is more than guesswork.

ASSURE, ENSURE or INSURE

These three verbs, all containing some idea of 'guarantee', are related but have different applications.

To **assure** is to 'guarantee', to 'give certainty to someone':

✓ They did their best to assure him that he was welcome.

To **ensure** is to 'make something safe or certain':

✓ Careful preparation helped to ensure the success of the expedition.

To **insure** is to 'protect oneself (financially) against loss or damage':

✓ We've insured the car.

AUGER or AUGUR

An **auger** (noun only) is an 'instrument for boring holes', usually in wood. An **augur** is a 'fortune-teller', the word deriving from the ancient Roman practice of telling the future through bird flights (which were seen as auguries).

AURAL or ORAL

Aural means 'of the ear'.

Oral means 'relating to the mouth'.

AVENGE or REVENGE

To **avenge** means to 'look for retribution' for a harm done not to the avenger but to somebody close to him/her.

To **revenge** is to 'harm in exchange for wrong done to oneself'.

B

BAIL or BALE

Bail is a noun and verb with several meanings. An accused person will obtain bail, or be bailed, in court, i.e. 'gain release from custody before trial by providing some security' (usually financial) which will forfeit if the defendant disappears. To bail also means to 'clear water out of' something, and to 'parachute out of an aircraft'. And finally, cricket stumps are topped by bails.

Bale can also be used as a verb in two of the senses above (baling water; baling out of a crashing aircraft). As a noun bale means a 'bundle' (a bale of cotton); as a verb, to 'do up in bundles' (baling hay).

BALMY or BARMY

Balmy (from balm, a healing ointment) means 'gentle', 'soothing'.

Barmy derives from barm, the froth on the head of fermenting liquor. So it means 'frothy' and therefore 'foolish', 'not right in the head'.

BENEFICENT BENEFICIAL, BENEVOLENT or BENIGN

Beneficent is a fairly high-flown word meaning 'kind or charitable' and tends to describe people and their actions or outlook.

Beneficial can mean simply 'useful', as in 'a beneficial exchange of views', but its most usual context is probably to do with 'promoting health or well-being'.

Benign, with the sense of 'kindly', is more to do with attitude than action (a benign smile, a benign presence) and has a special sense in describing a 'non-cancerous' growth - the opposite of 'malign! malignant'.

BEREAVED or BEREFT

Bereaved means 'deprived of by death', and should be used only about those who were genuinely close to the dead person. **Bereft** (originally having the same meaning as bereaved) generally means 'deprived of something or somebody significant', without having a necessary reference to death.

BESIDE or BESIDES

These two everyday words are often used as though they were completely interchangeable. They aren't.

Beside means 'next to' ('the table stood beside the window'). Besides **means** 'in addition to' ('besides the table, the room contained several chairs') and 'apart from' ('besides the table and chairs, the room was empty'). Besides, generally followed by a comma, also has the sense of 'moreover' ('Besides, there was nothing to be seen in the room ').

BIANNUAL or BIENNIAL

Biannual means 'occurring twice a year'.

Biannual ought not to be used to mean 'occurring every two years'.

Biennial means 'occurring every two years' and describes festivals or conferences which conform to this pattern or, as a noun, it applies to a 'plant which flowers or fruits only in its second year'.

BIAS or PREJUDICE

Bias is a milder form of prejudice.

A **prejudice** is an 'already formed opinion or reaction', i.e. one which isn't reasoned but usually emotional or instinctive.

BIZARRE or BAZAAR

Bizarre means 'odd to the point of being fantastically strange'.

A **bazaar** is a 'market-place' but it carries exotic overtones of crowded muddle.

BLOND or BLONDE

Blond, meaning 'fair', 'light-coloured', applies almost exclusively to hair colour. Both noun and adjective take the final 'e' if the subject is female.

When the word is applied to a masculine subject it should, strictly speaking, be spelled without the 'e'.

BON VIVANT or BON VIVEUR

A **bon viveur** is a 'pleasure-lover', a 'man about town'.

The term **bon vivant** is used in France with the meaning of 'jovial'.

BORN or BORNE

Borne is the past participle form of the verb to bear. It is applied to the carrier.

✓ She had borne him four children.

Otherwise the correct form is **born**.

BREACH or BREECH

A **breach** is an 'opening'.

Breech describes the 'part of a gun behind the barrel' or the 'back or buttocks' (hence breech delivery, when the baby emerges buttocks- or feet-first).

BRIDAL or BRIDLE

Bridal means 'relating to a bride'. A **bridle** is 'part of a horse's headgear, and therefore 'anything which restrains'. A bridle path is one on which horses can be led or ridden.

BROACH or BROOCH

Broach, a verb, generally occurs in two contexts: to broach a topic, to 'introduce' it into conversation, often with the suggestion of difficulty; less often — to broach a bottle (i.e. 'open' it).

Brooch, a noun, is an 'ornamental clasp'.

C

CALENDAR, CALENDER or COLANDER

A **calendar** is a 'table for telling the date' or simply a 'list'.

But **calender** is a word not in everyday use since it's restricted to a couple of specialist applications: a 'machine for rolling cloth or paper' or (still more obscure) a 'member of a Persian religious sect'.

Neither word should be confused with **colander,** the 'kitchen container used for straining food':

CALLOUS or CALLUS

Callous (which can be used to describe 'hardened' skin) is an adjective with the principal meaning of 'without feeling', or 'ruthless'.

Callus, which comes direct from Latin, is the noun for a 'patch of toughened skin'.

CAN or MAY

Can denotes ability:

✓ She can speak five languages.

but is often used in the sense of 'has permission':

✓ She's just been told she can come on the trip.

May indicates possibility:

✓ It may rain tomorrow.

and permission:

✓ You may leave when the job's finished.

CANNON or CANON

A **cannon** is a 'large gun' or a 'type of shot in billiards'.

Canon has a variety of different applications: a 'priest attached to a cathedral'; a 'principle or rule' (as in 'accepted canons of decency'); the 'body of work attributed to a particular author' (the Shakespearean canon, for example, covers all those works considered to have been written by him and not attributable to another author). Canon also has an adjectival form, 'canonical'.

CANVAS or CANVASS

Canvas is 'material used for painting on, for making ship sails', etc.; its plural form is 'canvases'.

To **canvass** (verb) is to 'gather support in a political setting' or simply to 'ascertain other people's views'.

Canvass also operates as a noun with the same sense of 'estimating numbers', 'gathering support for a vote'.

CAPITAL or CAPITOL

Capital has a range of meanings as a noun describing an 'important city' or 'seat of government', 'invested money', and generally 'stock'. As an adjective it means 'principal', 'connected to the head', 'involving the death penalty', etc.

Capitol, on the other hand, has a very restricted meaning, originally describing just two imperial edifices: 'the temple to Jupiter in ancient Rome' (built on the Capitoline hill) and 'the area in Washington, D.C. where the Senate and Congress are sited', also on a hill. Capitol is slightly stressed on the last syllable.

CAPTIVATE or CAPTURE

To **captivate** is to 'fascinate', to 'enchant':

To **capture** is to 'gain control of'. Although frequently used in a neutral sense ('to capture someone's attention') it also carries the meaning of to 'seize by force':

✓ The prisoner was captured after five hours on the run.

CARAT or CARET

A **carat** is a 'unit of weight used for assessing precious stones and gold'.

The quality of gold in an alloy measured in carats, each carat being one twenty-fourth of the total - hence 24-carat gold is pure gold. (The US spelling is usually karat.)

A **caret** is a 'symbol used in writing or proof reading showing where to insert something that has been left out'. It does look something like the tip of a carrot, perhaps, but that is only to add another layer of confusion.

CAVALRY or CALVARY

Cavalry is used to describe the 'troops who fought on horseback' and is now applied to the 'armoured and motorised part of an army'. **Calvary** was the 'place near Jerusalem where Christ was crucified'.

CELIBATE or CHASTE

Celibate is an adjective or noun which describes someone 'unmarried'.

Chaste doesn't have to mean 'going without sex', although this is generally implied. It carries the sense of 'modest', 'restrained'.

CENSORED or CENSORIOUS

Both these words derive from **censor**, but the meaning of the second has more in common with the meaning of censure.

Censored describes a book, play, film, etc. from which material has been cut on grounds of taste, potential for causing offence and so on. The word also applies to the excluded material.

CENTENARY or CENTENNIAL

Centenary (noun and adjective) is a British English usage meaning a 'hundred-year anniversary'. **Centennial** is a rare adjective meaning 'happening once in a hundred years'.

CEREAL or SERIAL

Cereal is 'edible grain' (barley, wheat, etc.). As an adjective **serial** means 'occurring in a series' (serial number, serial killings); as a noun, it applies to the 'episodes in a continuing story' in a magazine, on TV etc. This word implies a stronger degree of continuity than series.

CEREMONIAL or CEREMONIOUS

Both adjectives derive from ceremony but they have different meanings and applications.

Ceremonial means 'with the proper ceremony or ritual'.

By contrast, **ceremonious** conveys a note of criticism and means 'over- concerned with ceremony' and therefore 'pompous'.

CHAFE or CHAFF

To **chafe** — pronounced with a long 'a' - is to 'fret or wear by rubbing'. It can have a physical application (chafed skin) or a mental one. If a person **chafes** (at, against or under something) it means that he/she is resentful and uncomfortable on account of some external circumstance.

CHAOTIC or INCHOATE

Chaotic is obvious enough, having the meaning of 'very confused'.

Although something which is newly started may also be jumbled, even **chaotic**, there is a distinction between the two words and the writer ought to be certain of the sense in which he/she means it.

Inchoate means just begun; undeveloped.

CHILDISH or CHILDLIKE

Childish is used about adults in a critical sense, and describes behaviour which is 'non-adult', 'petulant', 'spoilt'.

Childlike is also applied to adults but this time often in approval, as it describes not so much behaviour as responses such as surprise and delight, or qualities like simplicity and trust — things that allegedly come more easily to children. **Childlike** is the opposite of 'worldly', 'cynical'.

CHRONIC or ACUTE

Chronic means 'long-lasting'. In itself a neutral word, it is almost always linked to some ongoing problem, as in 'chronic poverty', 'chronic back pain'.

Acute means 'sharp', 'urgent' — an acute illness is one which occurs suddenly and lasts a short time but may be life-threatening. Although a chronic condition will almost certainly be an unpleasant one, it does not necessarily endanger the life of the sufferer.

CLASSIC or CLASSICAL

Classic indicates that whatever is being described is an 'outstanding' example of its type or, at least, a 'highly representative' one: a book, film, song, dress, car etc. may be 'classic'.

As a plural noun, the term 'the classics' generally has a bit of dignity and weight; it is applied to works of art (most frequently literature and music created before 1900) which have lasted and achieved the status of intellectual and cultural touchstones.

Classical is an adjective originally describing 'anything relating to the Roman and ancient Greek period' — history, literature, studies.

CLIENT or CUSTOMER

A **client** is (or sounds) slightly more upmarket than a customer, being a 'person who consults/employs a professional adviser'. Surgeons, lawyers and financial consultants have clients. A **customer** was once merely 'someone who buys something', or a 'regular visitor to a shop'. It still means this, of course, but recently the customer has become a very exalted figure.

CLIMATIC or CLIMACTIC

Climatic is the adjective from 'climate':
✓ Climatic changes such as the earlier arrival of spring are a likely sign of global warming.

Climactic is the adjective from 'climax' and means 'culminating', 'most exciting'.

CLIMAX or CRESCENDO

Climax means 'culmination' and applies to the end-point and/or the most exciting moments in music, books, films and other forms of story-telling and sex. No difficulty with the definition of climax. **Crescendo** used in its correct sense of meaning 'increasing loudness'.

More usual is the application of crescendo to mean 'climax' or 'highpoint'.

CODA or CODICIL

A **coda** is a musical term describing a 'passage which brings a piece to a satisfactory end'. So it comes to apply to anything which makes a 'fitting conclusion'.

A **codicil** is primarily an 'addition to a will'.

COLLUDE, CONNIVE or CONSPIRE

To **collude** is to 'conspire with', especially in fraud.

To **connive**, meaning to 'plot', is a less critical term. It can suggest turning a blind eye to another's unofficial or illicit activities, or working together in underhand activities.

Conspire, once again to 'plot', is the strongest of these three terms and tends to be restricted to criminal contexts.

COME or -CUM-

Cum (the Latin for 'with') is used as a link word to show a double position or function: cook-cum-proprietor; cafe-cum-bar.

COMMON or MUTUAL

Common means 'shared', 'held jointly', as in common knowledge. **Mutual** describes something which is 'reciprocated'.

COMPARE or CONTRAST

To **compare** is to 'put things side by side and look for similarities'.

To **contrast** is to 'look for differences'.

COMPLACENT or COMPLAISANT

Complacent means 'pleased', 'satisfied with a situation as it is'. **Complaisant** means 'wanting to fall in with the wishes of others'.

COMPLEMENT or COMPLIMENT

As a noun **complement** is the 'number which will make complete' (as in a 'ship's complement') or an 'addition which makes for rightness or wholeness':

✓ For the British, chips are the right complement to fried fish.

Compliment, whether noun or verb, is 'praise':

✓ She complimented him on his skill in cooking.

COMPRISE or CONSIST

Both **comprise** and **consist** mean to 'include', to 'be formed of', but consist is always followed by 'of' or 'in':

✓ The New Testament consists of 27 books.

✓ The New Testament comprises 27 books.

'Comprised of' is frequently found but still wrong.

CONFIDENT or CONFIDANT

Confident means 'self-assured', 'trusting':

A **confidant** is a 'person in whom secrets are confided' and therefore a trusted friend.

CONGENIAL or GENIAL

Congenial and **genial** both carry the general sense of 'friendly', but congenial tends to be applied to surroundings and atmospheres rather than to individuals. It also means 'sympathetic' or 'suitable'.

Genial is used about people and means 'pleasant', 'cheerful'.

CONSEQUENT or CONSEQUENTIAL

Consequent means simply 'following on from':

✓ The share price fell by some 16 per cent on the consequent scams.

Consequential can be used in the sense of 'resulting from' but its more usual meaning is 'significant'.

CONTAGIOUS or INFECTIOUS

A **contagious** condition is spread 'by direct contact' — all sexually transmitted diseases, for example, are contagious. An **infectious** condition (e.g. flu) is 'carried by microbes through air or water'. When applied metaphorically to something which is 'quickly spreading' — enthusiasm, panic — either word can be used.

CONTEMPTIBLE or CONTEMPTUOUS

Contemptible means despicable, 'worthy of contempt'.

Contemptuous describes a person 'who shows contempt', is 'scornful'.

CONTINUOUS or CONTINUAL

Continual also indicates something 'lasting over a period but with breaks or interruptions' and so means 'repeated'.

(The same distinction applies to the adverbs continuously and continually.)

Continuous means 'occurring without interruption':

✓ We had continuous rain for 24 hours.

CONTRADICTION or PARADOX

A **contradiction** is a 'denial' in speech or an 'inconsistency' in a viewpoint.

If you contradict yourself you may be accused of fuzzy thinking, but to express a **paradox** suggests a more ingenious and agile state of mind since it is a 'statement which appears to be contradictory but which, when examined more closely, contains some truth'. A contradiction usually arises by accident; a paradox is the deliberate formulation of an unusual point of view.

CORRESPONDENT or CO-RESPONDENT

A **correspondent** is a 'letter-writer' or a 'journalist with a particular field of expertise' (e.g. an arts correspondent or sports correspondent).

A **co-respondent** (sometimes spelled without a hyphen) is the 'man or woman cited in a divorce case as the third party'.

CORROSIVE or CORUSCATING

Corrosive means 'eating away', and so gradually destroying. It can be used literally or metaphorically.

Coruscating comes from 'coruscate' and means 'sparkling'. It may be used literally (e.g. the effect of sunlight on water) but its most frequent application is metaphorical.

COUNCIL or COUNSEL

A **council** is an 'official group of people'; this is a noun only and is most often found in the context of local government.

Counsel is both a noun and a verb and carries the sense of 'advice or advising', often with a professional aspect to it.

Counsel also has the more specialised meaning of a 'courtroom lawyer'.

CREDIBLE, CREDITABLE or CREDULOUS

Three words connected with ideas of belief and trust, but with quite different meanings.

Credible means 'believable':

✓ He had some extraordinary things to say but his quiet manner made them credible.

The adjective is very widely used now to suggest not so much that something exists (i.e. is not a fiction), but that it should be taken seriously, as in 'a credible fighting force'. (The associated noun is credibility with the sense of 'believability').

Creditable means 'worth praising', with the slight suggestion that whatever is to be praised has been achieved in difficult circumstances:

✓ Despite her injury, she put up a very creditable performance.

(The noun equivalent is credit with the sense of 'honour', 'worth', and frequently with a financial application, as in credit limit, credit facilities, etc.)

Credulous means 'easily deceived', too 'ready to accept whatever people say.'

CRITERION or CRITERIA

A **criterion** is a 'standard for judging' or a 'test', suggesting a level you must reach in order to qualify for something:

✓ The criterion for selection is specified.

The plural is criteria (never 'criterias'):

✓ They are based on criteria including innovation, financial soundness and long-term investment value.

CURRANT or CURRENT

As a noun a **current** is a 'stream of air or water'. As an adjective **current** means 'of the present time' (as in 'current affairs'). A **currant** is a 'small dried grape', a 'raisin'.

D

DECRY or DESCRY

Decry means to 'condemn',

To **descry** is to 'find out something by looking'. It can be used of literal vision but is also used metaphorically for an attempt to peer into the future.

DE FACTO or DE JURE

This pair of Latin phrases is usually found together but they are opposites and shouldn't be confused. **De facto** means 'in fact', 'actually', and applies to the situation that exists without regard to what is rightful or what the law says about it. In contrast, **de jure** means 'by right', 'according to law'.

DEFECTIVE or DEFICIENT

Defective means 'faulty', 'badly made', 'not working to full effect', and can apply to body parts ('defective genes') as well as gadgets or merchandise.

Deficient means 'falling short', 'lacking in some way'.

DEFER or DELAY

This is a shade-of-meaning distinction but one which is worth noting.

Defer and **delay**, both meaning to 'put off', can be used almost interchangeably but there is also a difference of emphasis:

✓ Our visit was deferred can mean not only that the visit was delayed but that it was put off until a later and specified time, often as a result of a conscious decision on our part.

Defer followed by 'to' also has the sense of 'submit', 'give way to':

✓ The board was compelled to defer to the wishes of the majority shareholders.

DEFINITE or DEFINITIVE

Definite means 'exact', 'not vague':

✓ Have you got any definite plans for the summer?

Definitive means 'decisive', 'final'.

Definitive also carries the sense of 'setting a standard'.

DEFUSE or DIFFUSE

Defuse can be used only as a verb and means, literally, to 'take the fuse out' (of a bomb) or, figuratively, to 'bring calm into a tense situation':

✓ That's to say, making his life more comfortable, but also defusing his violent tendencies.

Diffuse as a verb means to 'scatter or spread through something or over a large area'

DELIVERANCE or DELIVERY

Deliverance is a literary word meaning 'liberation', setting free sometimes from a literal imprisonment but more often from a difficult or painful state of affairs. It is occasionally used as a euphemism for death.

Delivery also contains the idea of releasing or giving up, which turns into the notion of 'distribution'. Delivery is a bit of a buzzword at the moment, very popular in government handouts, company mission statements and other.

DEMUR or DEMURE

A verb and an adjective which look alike: They are not connected, although both have a suggestion of mildness about them. A fairly unusual word, **demur** — pronounced to rhyme with 'purr' — means to 'disagree with'. It does not suggest a violent objection, and is often found with 'not' as if to indicate that the speaker didn't feel strongly enough to disagree.

Demure — rhyming with 'pure' — is an adjective which means 'modest', with the suggestion of primness.

DEPENDANT or DEPENDENT

These two, one a noun, the other an adjective, comes in getting the ending right. Though spelled slightly differently they sound the same, hence the confusion.

Dependant is a noun only and describes 'someone who depends on another for support' (usually financial):

✓ She had four dependants, including her aged mother.

Dependent is an adjective meaning 'contingent', 'relying on':

✓ The college placement is dependent on his results.

DEPRECATE or DEPRECIATE

Two very similar words, both carrying the idea of 'running down, placing a low value on'.

Deprecate is more forceful than depreciate, and means to 'disapprove strongly of', to 'protest against'.

To **depreciate** is to 'go down in value':
✓ No car salesman is likely to depreciate his own products.

DERISIVE or DERISORY

Derisive means 'showing (humorous) contempt for'.

To describe something as **derisory** means that it is absurdly inadequate and can justifiably be treated with a dismissive laugh because it is 'worth deriding'.

DESERT or DESSERT

Quite similar pronunciation and uncertainty over the doubling of 's' can cause confusion between this familiar pair.

Desert is a 'dry sandy place' and, collectively, they—the Sahara, the Kalahari, etc.—are deserts.

An altogether different word, with the same spelling but a different pronunciation stressing the second syllable, is desert with the meaning of 'what one deserves'. This term, usually in the plural, has a negative ring. To get one's deserts, almost invariably just deserts, is to receive the unpleasant consequences of unpleasant actions.

Dessert - also pronounced with the stress on the second syllable - is the 'last course in a meal'.

DEVIANT or DEVIOUS

Deviant means 'departing from what is normal'. When used as a noun, the word almost always has a sexual application, a deviant being one step short of a 'pervert', at least in tabloid-speak.

Devious can mean 'winding' when describing such things as roads but a much more usual application is to people, where it means 'cunning'.

DIAGNOSIS or PROGNOSIS

One word looks backwards, the other forward.

Diagnosis can be used more generally, the original meaning of the word refers to the 'identification of a medical condition through its symptoms'

The **prognosis** can only take place after the diagnosis since it is the 'forecast of the likely development' (of the disease or condition). Both words are often used outside a medical context, diagnosis to mean simply an 'analysis' and prognosis a 'prediction':

DISCOMFIT or DISCOMFORT

These words have different roots in French and Latin, but they look alike and one often leads to another — if you're discomfited you'll probably feel some mental or physical discomfort as well. So it's quite hard to draw a line between them.

Discomfit (verb) is to 'disconcert', to 'embarrass', with the sense of being put on the spot.

(The associated noun is discomfiture.)

As a verb **discomfort** literally means to 'deprive of comfort', though in practice it is used in the same meaning as discomfit.

DISCREET or DISCRETE

These two words, originally derived from the same Latin

word, are pronounced identically and also share the idea of 'keeping apart'.

But they have acquired quite different meanings.

Discreet is used almost always in the sense of 'being able to keep secrets or confidences' and therefore 'careful or tactful'.

The frequent confusion between these two may be made worse by the fact that the noun from discreet, **'discretion'**, looks uncommonly as if it's derived from discrete.

DISCRIMINATING or DISCRIMINATORY

Both of these words derive from **discriminate**, but the meaning of one is positive, the other negative.

As an adjective, **discriminating** is usually complimentary since it describes a person who is capable of 'showing good judgment' (often in relation to food and drink).

Discriminatory is generally negative since it carries the sense of 'prejudiced' (because a particular group is being picked out or discriminated against on grounds of race, gender, etc.)

DISINTERESTED or UNINTERESTED

Two words which sound similar and which everyday use has made into equivalents. But precise definitions and careful usage say otherwise.

To take the one with the obvious meaning first: **uninterested** means 'bored by', 'not attracted to':

✓ Few newspaper readers are uninterested in the private lives of public figures.

The original meaning of **disinterested** is 'neutral', 'impartial'. Correctly, this is the sense in which it's used here:

✓ Then I was reminded of my childhood. It was a time when politicians were all deemed to be disinterested public servants.

DISTIL or INSTIL

Two words, with identical endings and with vague 'chemical' overtones, whose meanings may sometimes be confused.

To **distil** (spelled with a double 'll' in the US) is to 'produce in concentrated form'. The word describes a chemical process for producing spirits, perfumes, etc. but is frequently applied to any attempt to reach the essence of a situation.

To **instil** is to 'introduce slowly or drop by drop'.

DISTINCT, DISTINCTIVE or DISTINGUISHED

These adjectives, containing the idea of something 'standing out', tend to run into one another but they have separate functions.

Distinct means 'standing out', 'noticeable':

✓ There's a distinct smell of gas in the kitchen.

To describe something as **distinctive** suggests that it is 'typical or characteristic' of a person or place.

Distinguished means 'eminent', 'worthy of respect':

✓ After a distinguished period as Foreign Secretary, he retired to write novels.

DOMINANT or DOMINEERING

Both of these similar-sounding words are to do with control

but the first can be more or less neutral while the second always implies a criticism.

Dominant is 'leading', 'commanding', and can be applied to people, countries, styles, etc.

Domineering is almost always used about individuals, and means 'overbearing', 'bullying'.

DOWNSTAGE or UPSTAGE

Downstage describes the 'area of the stage closest to the audience' while **upstage** is the 'area farthest away from the audience'.

To **upstage** someone, inside or outside the theatre, is to 'draw attention away from that person to oneself' (since an actor moving upstage may force the other actors to turn towards him, hence putting their backs to the audience).

DRAFT or DRAUGHT

These words are very easily confused. They are pronounced the same, and both are connected to different senses of 'draw'.

Draft has the sense of 'something drawn'. As a noun it is a 'first version' of something like a plan or document, and as a verb it means to 'produce a rough, early version':

✓ He drafted the outline of his speech on the back of an envelope.

By contrast, a **draughtsman** is 'someone who works with designs or pictures'. The word **draught** is more concerned with the 'act of drawing'.

DUAL or DUEL

Two identically pronounced words which are quite easily confused, perhaps suggested by the idea of the 'two' sides involved in a duel.

Dual is an adjective meaning 'twofold': **dual** controls, a dual personality:

✓ The briefcase, however, serves a dual purpose. It holds documents.

Duel is a noun or verb indicating an 'arranged fight between two individuals'.

DUE TO or OWING TO

Due to, meaning 'on account of', should be used only in an adjectival sense, so that it is actually qualifying a noun:

✓ The outbreak of food poisoning was probably due to the stale chicken.

The different applications of **due to/owing to** are not observed by many people.

E

EATABLE or EDIBLE

If something is **edible** then it is 'safe to eat', that is, it won't poison you:

✓ Many kinds of mushroom are not edible.

Eatable then it is 'fit to eat', even quite good — but the word does not convey much enthusiasm and you wouldn't use it as a compliment on someone's cooking.

ECONOMIC or ECONOMICAL

These two terms are frequently used as if they amounted to the same thing but there is a gap between their meanings.

Economic means 'relating to the economy', and can be used on several levels from the global or the national down to the personal.

Economical is an altogether more homely term, and when applied to an individual means 'careful with money' (with a hint of stinginess); when used about products it suggests that the consumer is getting value for money:

✓ This is an economical car: it averages 24 km per litre.

Economical can also suggest 'sparing', 'small in quantity' (an economical portion).

EERIE or EYRIE

Any confusion between these two arises because of uncertainty over their spelling rather than meaning.

The adjective **eerie** (sometimes eery) describes something which is 'strange', 'unsettling'. The word can have supernatural overtones but it generally seems to be used as a synonym for 'weird'.

An **eyrie** — which has variant spellings such as aerie — is the 'nest of an eagle' (or any bird of prey) but is more commonly used to describe 'any high and secure place'.

EFFECTIVE, EFFECTUAL or EFFICACIOUS

These words are very close - all having the sense of 'producing a result' — but they appear in slightly different contexts.

Effective tends to be used of people and things in the sense of 'having an impact', 'producing the desired result':

✓ Cigarette companies recently agreed to put more effective warnings on the packets.

Effectual is a much less usual word meaning essentially the same (and more frequently found in its negative form of ineffectual):

✓ The new warnings on tobacco products were effectual in reducing sales.

Efficacious also means 'capable of producing the intended result', but its use is almost entirely confined to medicines and remedies.

E.G. or I.E

The common abbreviations e.g. and i.e. (almost always appearing in lower case, and sometimes without full stops) are short for Latin phrases and are occasionally confused, through a misunderstanding of their individual functions.

The abbreviation **e.g.** (exempli gratia — 'for example') introduces an example, one or two out of several.

In contrast **i.e.** (ildest - 'that is') introduces an explanation or amplification of a previous statement:

✓ Each bird is easily divided into four. First, gently pull the leg (i.e. drumstick and thigh) away from the body.

ELDER or OLDER

People sense vaguely that there is some difference between these almost identical terms but are not sure what it is.

Of these two adjectives in the comparative form (the superlatives are eldest and oldest), **older** can be used in almost any context (an older person, an older car) while **elder** should be restricted to people, generally within a family framework (my elder sister). Elder also has the noun sense of 'someone who should be looked up to', on account of their years of experience, as in 'elders and betters' (although it's hard to imagine this phrase being used now without a trace of irony).

ELECTRIC, ELECTRICAL or ELECTRIFYING

Only one of these words is usually applied in a literal sense, but which?

All these terms derive from **'electricity'** but **electric** is used in a figurative sense to mean 'exciting' or 'startling' (an electric performance; an electric intervention in a debate) as well as in its literal application (electric light). **Electrical** simply means 'related to electricity' and is applied to supplies, faults, etc. (an electrical breakdown). The adjective **electrifying** is almost always used in the figurative sense of electric but carries an even stronger charge: 'astonishing'.

ELEGY or EULOGY

Two words that sound similar and which, in their origins, describe speeches or poems delivered on significant occasions.

An **elegy** was originally a 'song or poem of mourning'. Now it tends to be used as anything which takes a nostalgic or melancholy look back at the past.

A **eulogy** can also be delivered at a Funeral since it means a 'speech of praise', but it is frequently found in lighter contexts.

(The associated adjectives are elegiac — often employed to describe pictures, music, moods, etc., and meaning no more than 'pleasantly sad' — and eulogistic.)

ELICIT or ILLICIT

These words may be confused because they sound almost identical but in fact they have nothing to do with each other.

The verb **elicit** means to 'evoke' or 'draw out'.

The adjective **illicit** means 'not allowed', 'unlawful'. The word carries a stealthy overtone, but is less forceful than 'illegal'.

ELOQUENCE or LOQUACITY

Each of these terms is connected to speech, one in a positive way, the other negative.

Eloquence is 'persuasive, flowing speech'.

Loquacity is 'talkativeness'. It tends to be used in a pejorative sense.

(The related adjectives are loquacious and eloquent. This second word can apply to other things apart from speech — a gesture can be eloquent [i.e. 'expressive'])

EMINENT, IMMINENT or IMMANENT

The first two words are close in pronunciation, the last two even more so. The first carries the idea of importance, the second implies urgency so some confusion is perhaps natural. The last word is quite rare but is sometimes confused with the second.

Eminent means 'conspicuous', 'distinguished', and is usually applied to people.

Imminent means 'about to happen'.

Immanent is a fairly rare adjective with a philosophical meaning of 'pervading', 'inherent'.

(The noun forms are eminence, imminence and immanence, respectively.)

EMOTIONAL or EMOTIVE

Both words are obviously connected to emotion, but have different applications.

Emotional tends to be used in the sense of 'excitable' or 'moody'. The word sometimes has a slightly critical edge to it.

Emotive means 'intended to stir the emotions'. It's usually applied to language and sometimes to images which set out to manipulate an audience by triggering certain responses:

✓ It was a highly emotive advertisement.

EMPATHY or SYMPATHY

Both nouns are to do with feeling, and probably because they describe somewhat amorphous reactions, they tend to blur into each other. However they have fairly different applications which are worth preserving.

Empathy is 'imaginative identification with someone else' and his or her situation, whether that situation is a good or bad one.

Sympathy also involves the attempt to see things from the perspective of another person and carries the additional sense of 'compassion'.

(The related verbs are empathise and sympathise.)

EMULATE or IMITATE

Both of these terms are to do with 'copying' and are sometimes used interchangeably. But their associations are quite different and worth noting.

To **emulate** is to **'imitate'** but it carries more positive overtones than the second word because the idea of rivalry is often involved rather than mere copying. Therefore to emulate is also to 'try to equal or outdo'.

To **imitate** is simply to 'copy'. The word frequently has negative associations — imitations are much more often described as poor than good.

ENDEMIC, EPIDEMIC or PANDEMIC

Three terms which are widely linked to outbreaks (of disease) and their spread. The differences between them are sometimes blurred.

Endemic, an adjective, means 'widely found among a certain group or in a certain area', and although often referring to disease it can extend to other topics.

Epidemic is a noun or adjective describing an 'outbreak' — usually of a disease (though one could talk of an epidemic of panic). A characteristic of an epidemic is that it is relatively short-lived, unlike something endemic, which is likely to be there for good.

ENORMITY or ENORMOUSNESS

Two words both deriving from enormous and suggesting size, although the principal meaning of the first word is connected to crimes of great magnitude. (The Latin root of enormous indicates something which has deviated from the rule or norm.)

The first word in this pair is definitely the more widely used of the two, whatever the context. Strictly speaking, there is a distinction, since the noun enormity characterises 'extreme wickedness' or an 'outrage':

✓ The enormity of Hitler's crimes had been exposed.

The preference for enormity, when what is really meant is **enormousness,** may have something to do with the slightly cumbersome quality of the longer word, and there are contexts when the two senses do seem to blur together

ENQUIRY or INQUIRY

The different spellings of this word maybe appropriate in particular contexts.

Inquiry tends to be used for an official investigation, where the word is usually capitalized, but the general preference is to use the other spelling in such contexts as 'enquiries welcomed'.

(Most dictionaries simply list **'enquiry'** as a variant spelling of 'inquiry'. US usage favours 'inquiry'.)

ENVELOP or ENVELOPE

Confusion arises over the spelling of these two, with a tendency to use the more familiar second word in all contexts. Moreover this tendency has caused further confusion: the verb 'develop' is often misspelled as 'develope'.

To **envelop** is a verb meaning to 'cover' or 'wrap round'. It is not spelled with an 'e' at the end, and the stress falls in the middle of the word:

✓ Whatever the reason, it's become the second controversy to envelop her this year.

Envelope, with the stress falling on the beginning of the word, is a noun only and describes the 'thing which does the covering':

✓ He had to nerve himself to open the envelope from the Income Tax Department.

EQUABLE or EQUITABLE

Both of these adjectives contain ideas of balance and evenness, but they are found in different areas.

The adjective **equable** means 'even', 'without extremes'. Frequently applied to the weather, where it means much the same as 'temperate', it also describes character:

✓ He had such an equable temperament that it was impossible to pick a quarrel or an argument with him.

Equitable means 'just', 'following the principles of fairness'.

EROTIC or PORNOGRAPHIC

This isn't a confusion so much as a matter of definition or rather a question of point of view since the definition of both words is essentially 'arousing sexual desire'. **Pornographic** carries the additional, sense obscene'. But the words are constantly changing in this field, and what was yesterday's pornography becomes today's **eroticism.**

ESCAPEE, ESCAPER, ESCAPIST or ESCAPOLOGIST

The four words characterise the individual who seeks to get out of somewhere uncomfortable or confining, but each of them crops up in a different context.

An **escapee** is 'one who escapes'. The word almost always has a literal application to describe the person who gets out of a jail. An alternative form is escaper.

✓ An **escapist** is a 'person who is looking to escape from reality'. This word - most usually found as an adjective describing books, films and so on - doesn't necessarily carry a negative charge. But someone who gravitates towards escapist material all the time may not be in a healthy state of mind:

✓ He argues that the flood of books about fairies and angels is a symptom of escapist despair by people who feel impotent to improve their lives.

An escapologist is a 'person who repeatedly gets out of tricky situations'. Originally used about those showmen and magicians who made their living out of escaping from 'impossible' situations (involving chains, padlocks, barrels flung into rivers, and the rest), it's now applied to politicians.

(The related abstract nouns are escapism and escapology.)

ESPECIAL or SPECIAL

The adjectives especial and special, and the adverb forms (especially, specially), are used almost interchangeably although there is a useful distinction between them.

Especial and especially, meaning 'principal', 'very much', intensify whatever word they are linked with: an especial friend; an especially happy day.

Special is very often used in the sense of especial (a special friend, occasion, etc.) but it carries the additional sense of 'specific' or 'confined to a particular subject':

✓ I had a special reason for wanting to see you today.

Special can also be a noun: today's specials (on a menu).

(Especial should not be used in the sense of 'specific' shown above).

ESTIMATE or GUESSTIMATE

An **estimate** is a 'rough calculation' (notoriously rough in the case of builders' estimates and the like) or an 'attempt to judge the worth of anything'. A **guesstimate** is supposedly better than a 'guess' but less accurate than an 'estimate'.

EUPHEMISM or EUPHUISM

The unusual spelling of both these words means the second is sometimes mistakenly used when the first is meant.

A **euphemism** is a 'word or phrase which expresses a potentially offensive fact or truth in a more palatable way' — and that's an elaborate definition for an activity which all of us practise every day. Euphemisms tend to cluster around the embarrassing or threatening aspects of life: sex, death, bodily functions ('sleep with', 'pass on', 'spend a penny'). But even an innocent act like asking to 'borrow' sugar from a neighbour — do people still do that? — could be called a euphemism since what's usually meant is 'have'. More often, however, a euphemism is designed to blur the truth and can come close to being a lie.

By contrast, **euphuism,** sometimes used in error for euphemism, has a very restricted application since it defines a 'high-flown, extravagant style of writing' which was in vogue at the end of the 16th century.

EVERY DAY or EVERYDAY

These two are not identical and the distinction between them - one which is plainer in writing than in speech - should be kept.

Every day means just that, 'occurring daily':

- ✓ Looking back, it seemed as though the sun shone every day that summer.

Everyday (one word) means 'ordinary' — since something that happens every day soon becomes usual:

- ✓ The benefits of the everyday application of superconductivity in the medical, industrial and scientific fields are incalculable.

EVERY ONE or EVERYONE

As with the previous distinction between 'every day' and

'everyday', this one is more obvious in writing than in speaking, where the words naturally run together.

Every one is chiefly used of things:

✓ Dozens of used cars — every one a bargain!

Everyone is only used of people:

✓ Everyone was shocked by the news.

Every one can be used of people in a more emphatic or specific context:

✓ There were quite a few people in the room and every one was shocked by the news.

EVIDENCE or EVINCE

Two similar-sounding words which involve ideas of displaying or proving.

Evidence is mainly found in its noun use (the evidence in the case) but it can also be used as a verb with the sense of to 'make evident', to 'show':

✓ Some people don't like — all right, I don't like — this verb use of evidence. It sounds awkward and a simple word like 'show' will do a better job.

Evince means to 'show clearly', and is used of people rather than figures, data, etc.:

✓ He never evinced much interest in investment or business transactions.

✓ It had been a poor year for the company, as evinced by the figures.

EXALTED or EXULTANT

A similar look to these two words, together with the idea of being at a kind of peak, may cause confusion.

Exalted (adjective) means 'high', 'dignified':

✓ Despite his exalted position, the President never lost touch with his roots.

Exultant (adjective) means 'triumphant'.

(The associated verbs are exalt and exult, while the noun forms are exaltation and exultation.)

EXCEPTIONAL or EXCEPTIONABLE

Both of these adjectives derive from the noun exception, which has the double meaning of 'something excluded' and an 'objection', and this is what causes the confusion. The second word is sometimes used for the first, perhaps because people think it sounds like an intensified form of exceptional.

Exceptional means 'outstanding', 'excluded from the normal run of things':

✓ That summer was exceptional for its low rainfall.

Exceptionable means 'objectionable' (i.e. it describes something to which exception could be taken).

EXHAUSTED, EXHAUSTING or EXHAUSTIVE

Because of its shared root in the verb exhaust, the third of these terms is sometimes confused with the second one.

Exhausted is simply 'very tired':

✓ Working for six months without a break left her totally exhausted.

Exhausting means 'very tiring':

✓ She found it exhausting to go for so long without a holiday.

Exhaustive means 'very thorough':
- ✓ When she came back she gave us an exhaustive account of her holidays.

EXHIBITER, EXHIBITIONER or EXHIBITIONIST

Quite different, these three, although ideas of 'showing off' link the first and last.

The term for a person who shows pictures, works, etc. at art exhibitions is an **exhibiter**. An **exhibitioner** is a 'university student awarded an exhibition' (i.e. a grant of money, usually made in recognition of academic achievement — this is an older and specialist meaning of exhibition). An **exhibitionist** is a 'person who likes showing off'. It also describes those people who expose themselves sexually in public. In this sense exhibitionist is a unisex term — although the slang equivalent, 'flasher', is generally applied only to men.

EXHORT or EXTORT

Two words, similar in shape and sound, which both carry overtones of force.

To **exhort** is to 'encourage' or 'urge' and there is usually a faintly bullying overtone to the word.

To **extort** is to 'obtain something (usually money) by violence or the threat of it':
- ✓ The protection gang extorted money from half the clubs in the city.

EXPLICIT or IMPLICIT

These adjectives are both applied to the meaning of something but in opposite senses.

The notice gave an **explicit** warning that shoplifters would be prosecuted. (**Explicit** is also the shorthand term for sexually frank language or action in the media. As such, it can operate as a warning or — more often, surely? — as an inducement to watch and listen.) **Implicit** means 'suggested', 'not openly stated'.

(**Implicit** also carries the sense of 'absolute', 'unquestioning': implicit trust.)

Explicit is 'frank', 'clear'.

EXTEMPORE or IMPROMPTU

Two words from Latin which are frequently used interchangeably although there are subtle differences of emphasis and application between them.

Extempore describes a speech, performance, etc. which is done 'off the cuff', 'without the help of notes' but not necessarily without any preparation.

Impromptu also applies to performances with the sense of 'unprepared', but it carries the additional meaning of 'makeshift' and can describe arrangements, structures and so on.

F

FACTIOUS or FRACTIOUS

These words not only look very similar but both contain the idea of 'troublesome'.

Factious — from 'faction', describing a small group (usually within a larger one) that has its own agenda — means 'inclined to form factions', 'trouble-seeking'.

Fractious means 'quarrelsome'. The word is generally applied to children. In some ways it's the junior version of factious:

✓ When the children get back from an outing, tired, fractious and hungry, it is essential to remove them to a safe place while you cook lunch.

FAINT or FEINT

Both words are pronounced the same. Any confusion is sometimes attributed to the fact that printers refer to the **faint** lines printed on some stationery as **feint**, although this term seems too specialised to have affected general usage.

As a verb **faint** means to 'lose consciousness briefly'; as an adjective it means 'not distinct', 'weak'. The word shouldn't be confused with **feint** (noun and verb) which describes a 'deceptive move made during a fight/battle to trick one's opponent' — usually to conceal the direction from which the real blow is coming.

FAIR or FARE

This is a pair of confusables, like 'bail/bale', with a raft of meanings attached.

Fair as a noun describes a 'market for business or pleasure'(antiques fair, tradefair, funfair). As an adjective, **fair** has a range of meanings from 'bright' (a fair day) to 'just' (a fair exchange) to the very English 'not bad' (fair marks). As a verb **fare** means to 'travel' or 'get on' — not much found now except in slightly quaint expressions like 'How are you faring?' As a noun a fare is the 'price of a journey' (train fare) or 'food/provisions', although this second sense seems restricted to supermarket advertising and the hospitality industry.

FANCIFUL, IMAGINARY or IMAGINATIVE

Three words associated with the word imagination but with widely differing meanings.

'**Fancy**' in its old sense is connected to the 'imagination', since it was regarded as a kind of younger brother, a bit wilder and more frivolous.

This historical sense has pretty well disappeared but the adjective **fanciful** occupies ground somewhere between imaginative and silly; best defined perhaps as 'unrealistic'.

Imaginary means 'having no basis in reality', 'illusory'.

FARTHER or FURTHER

Farther means the same as **further**, and is preferred by some people when physical distance is the topic because it looks as though it is the comparative form of 'far':

✓ We overtook them a few miles farther on.

✓ Inflation rose further than expected last month.

FAUN or FAWN

There is a link between these identically pronounced words in that both can refer to shy, perhaps skittish creatures. This is the probable reason for the confusion over spelling.

Faun has only one meaning: it describes a 'mythological creature with a man's body and a goat's legs, horns and a tail'. It - or he - should not be confused with fawn, a 'young deer', even though in a sense both fauns and fawns are woodland creatures.

Fawn is also a colour ('yellowish-brown') and, as a verb followed by 'over', means to 'flatter or show affection' — always used pejoratively.

FAZE or PHASE

Faze 'looks' like a new word although in fact it is found as early as the 19th century in the US, and it is perhaps people's unfamiliarity with the written form that causes them to substitute phase/phased.

To **faze** (it only appears as a verb and in the participle form fazed) is to 'shake up', to 'worry'.

Phase is a noun and a verb. As a noun, it describes a 'stage in the development of a person, organisation, etc.':

✓ Most teenagers go through a phase when they find their parents irritating.

As a verb, phase is usually coupled with 'in' or 'out', and describes a slow process in which something new appears or something old vanishes.

FEMININE, EFFEMINATE or EFFETE

Almost everyone is aware of the difference between the first two words, but many assume mistakenly that effete — probably because of the similarity of sound and the contexts in which the word often appears — means the same as effeminate.

Feminine means 'characteristic of women' and although used principally of women (obviously!) it can describe an attribute which a man might have: a feminine voice; a feminine sensitivity. **Effeminate,** only used of men, means 'woman-like' and so 'unmanly' - it's a pejorative term:

✓ He is quite effeminate in his ways.

Effete has nothing to do with effeminate but, by a rather complicated process, moves from meaning 'worn out' (originally through childbirth) to 'barren' to 'degenerate'. In fact, the usual application of the word is lighter than its serious history suggests and effete winds up meaning something between 'useless' and 'frivolous'.

FERAL or FEROCIOUS

There are fashions in words and it's my impression that feral has been growing more popular recently. There is some overlap of meaning with ferocious but the two words are not synonymous.

Feral means 'wild', 'not (or no longer) domesticated'. It can be applied to people and occasionally to someone's appearance (a feral child is one who has been 'brought up' by animals). But the usual context is animal life — cats, pigeons and so on:

✓ One student, Anita, told of her holiday fun: she goes hunting for feral pigs with her nine dogs.

Though the adjective **ferocious** can mean 'cruel', it is more often found in the sense of 'intense':

✓ The company founder has also launched a ferocious campaign against its competitor.

FEWER or LESS

These words are frequently swapped for each other in speech and writing but formal English makes a distinction between them.

Both of these adjectival comparatives (few/fewer; little/less) indicate a smaller number or quantity. **Fewer** should be used when referring to a number of objects or people (i.e. with a plural noun):

✓ There were fewer swimmers in the pool today.

Less should be applied to any singular item or unit:

✓ Diet experts advise us to put less salt in our food.

FIANCE or FIANCEE

Both words are now slightly formal terms for people who are engaged to be married and the ending is an indication of gender.

A **fiancé** is the 'husband-to-be'; a **fiancée** is the 'wife-to-be'. The first spelling is sometimes used for both sexes but the difference should be observed. (Each word takes an accent over the first 'e'.)

FLAIR or FLARE

Flair is a noun indicating a 'natural ability' in something (a flair for languages), while **flare** as a verb means to 'blaze out' or, as a noun, denotes a 'sudden light' (generally some kind of warning signal). It's this second spelling —**flares** — that describes the trousers of the 1970s, the decade when taste took a back seat. If the two words are confused it's usually because the second is used in error when the first is meant:

✓ He had a particular flare [should be flair] for recruiting new members.

FLAMMABLE, INFLAMMABLE or INFLAMMATORY

Ideas of 'going up in flames' underlie all three words but they have different uses. The first two words are interchangeable since the 'in-' prefix on the second does not turn it into a negative. The last term cannot be used in place of the other two.

The first two adjectives mean the same thing, 'capable of being (easily) set on fire'. The story goes that **flammable** was 'invented' because the 'in-' prefix on inflammable gave it the appearance of a negative (along the lines of 'visible/invisible'), thus suggesting that the object described could not be set on fire. Is there any recorded case of someone dropping a match on an item labelled **inflammable** and being surprised when it went up in flames? Nevertheless, flammable is the preferred alternative now.

Inflammatory should not be applied to the fire-raising properties of a substance but rather means 'rousing strong feelings'. It normally describes comments or articles that, intentionally or otherwise, spark a protest.

FLAUNT or FLOUT

To **flaunt** is to 'make a public exhibition of', to 'show off'. To **flout** is to 'treat something with contempt'; it's generally used when laws, rules, conventions are being disregarded — in a very public way:

✓ 'They flouted the law just to get publicity.'

FLOTSAM or JETSAM

Flotsam describes 'any item lost during a shipwreck and later found floating in the water'. **Jetsam** applies to 'items which are deliberately thrown overboard' (e.g. to lighten the ship). The pair almost always has a metaphorical application now.

FLOUNDER or FOUNDER

These two verbs, very similar in sound and with associated meanings, are often misused.

To **flounder** is to 'struggle', to 'stumble':

✓ Without his cue card he was floundering for something to say.

To **founder** means to 'fall in ruins', to 'sink', and might be seen as the next (and last) stage after floundering. The verb is sometimes applied to horses, who might founder on the home straight, but most often to ships and, in a figurative sense, to people's schemes.

FLU or FLUE

Flu is the familiar and shortened form of 'influenza' (from an Italian word for 'influence' and following the old idea that diseases were the result of the malign effect of the 'stars').

The two words are occasionally confused, with the result that people appear to suffer from a chimney disease:

✓ Withdrawal symptoms included nausea, flue (should be flu-) like symptoms, anxiety and sweating.

FOOLISH or FOOLHARDY

Both deriving from 'fool', these words carry distinct shades of meaning.

Foolish is applied to anybody or anything which the speaker or writer considers 'unwise or stupid'.

Foolhardy also means 'unwise' but with an overtone of 'impetuous' (i.e. foolish + hardy). There's sometimes a touch of admiration in the word when it carries the sense of 'risk-taking':

✓ The truly foolhardy can even stay the night in an arctic sleeping bag on an ice block bed.

FORBEAR or FOREBEAR

To **forbear** (with the stress falling on the second syllable) is to 'abstain', to 'hold back from'. The word is really for formal use, especially in its past tense form of forbore:

✓ He was severely criticised in the report but forbore from making a public response.

A **forebear** (which can also be spelled forbear but with the stress falling on the first syllable, regardless of spelling) is an 'ancestor', usually from several generations back.

FORBIDDING or FOREBODING

These words are different but they are both connected with the idea of threat, which is probably what causes any confusion.

Forbidding is an adjective with the sense of 'sinister', 'threatening' (usually in the appearance of people, buildings or places)

Foreboding is a noun which describes a 'feeling of unease'.

FORCEFUL, FORCIBLE or FORCED

Like many sets of adjectives which derive from a single noun, in this case force, the meanings of the individual words carry distinct shades of meaning.

Forceful, meaning 'with force' or 'vigorous', tends to be used about a person's character, attitude or words:

✓ He was a man of forceful personality and strong opinions.

Forcible can also be found in this sense of 'imposing' (a forceful/forcible speaker), but it more usually has a physical context and means 'employing force' - one step away from 'violent':

✓ The police made a forcible removal of the demonstrators from the scene.

Forced has a variety of meanings from 'strained' (a forced smile) to 'rapidly ripened' (forced fruit) and 'compelled' (forced removal).

FOREGO or FORGO

As with a number of word pairs beginning 'for-/fore-', it is easy to get confused over which form to use.

To **forego** is to 'go in front of'. It is hardly ever — or never — used except in the forms of foregoing and foregone (the foregoing points in an argument, a foregone conclusion).

To **forgo**, which has the alternative spelling forego, is to 'do without something':

✓ When his parents were away, he was obliged to forego his usual home food.

FOR EVER or FOREVER

As with 'every day/everyday' and 'every one/everyone', there is a slight and useful distinction between these two forms.

The one-word spelling can be used all the time — forever, one might say. But when 'eternally' is meant then the two-word for ever is preferred by some people:

✓ The universe won't last for ever, you know.

In the sense of 'continually', 'all the time', the one-word form should be used:

✓ It's forever raining round these parts.

FORMALLY or FORMERLY

The near-identical pronunciation of these two can cause problems over spelling.

Formally means 'in the proper style', 'officially':

✓ The recent Congress meeting formally adopted laws protecting private property rights.

Formerly means 'at an earlier time':

✓ The money set aside for good causes is now being spent on projects that would formerly have been paid for out of general expenses.

FORTH or FOURTH

A simple pair, but it is surprisingly easy to miss out the 'H' in fourth and so produce the wrong word.

Forth is an old word meaning 'forward' or 'outward'. It appears as a prefix in words such as forthcoming or forthright, but is not used by itself now except in the phrase 'and so forth' or in variants on the Biblical 'Go forth and multiply'. This spelling is sometimes used by mistake for **fourth**, referring to the number 4.

FORTUITOUS or FORTUNATE

Fortuitous has gradually been encroaching on the territory of **fortunate**, and it is frequently used in the sense of the second word although its primary meaning is different.

Strictly speaking, **fortuitous** means occurring by chance:

✓ They were just talking about him when he made a fortuitous appearance at the door.

Fortunate is 'lucky':

✓ She was fortunate to receive only mild punishment for her mistakes.

But the similarity between the two words means that fortuitous is generally used to suggest an element of (good) luck combined with chance.

FULSOME or HEARTFELT

These two are near opposites, yet the first word is sometimes used as if it meant the same as the second. It doesn't.

Fulsome is a tricky word to interpret because it often occurs in an ambiguous context. Meaning 'sickeningly admiring', it suggests hypocrisy.

But when fulsome is applied to, say, 'praise' or 'apology', it's not always clear whether the writer intends it in the (mistaken) sense of abundant, probably suggested by the *ful*-means prefix. If you want to convey sincerity then **heartfelt** is a better word, as it means what it says, i.e. 'deeply felt'.

G

GALLING or GRUELLING

A slight overlap in meaning and a similarity in sound sometimes cause these two to be confused.

Something which is **galling** is 'irritating'.

Gruelling means 'punishing', 'very tiring', and is applied to an experience or course which entails great physical or psychological stress.

GAMBIT, GAMUT or GAUNTLET

A **gambit** is an 'opening move', originally in chess (where the term is applied to the deliberate sacrifice of a piece to gain an advantage).

Now the term is extended to any 'thought-out manoeuvre which begins a game, negotiation, etc.'

GAMBLE or GAMBOL

Confusion between these two is a spelling error, not one of sense: pronunciation is no help here.

To **gamble** is to 'risk' or to 'play for money':

✓ Some come to gamble high stakes.

To **gambol** is to 'leap around playfully':

✓ Our pets need to be allowed to frolic and gambol.

(The past tense forms of each word are gambled and gambolled).

GARNER or GARNISH

These similar-sounding words are occasionally confused,

perhaps through some indirect link between ideas of food and harvest.

Connected to granary (a storehouse for grain), **garner** means to 'gather up':

✓ He has garnered particular critical acclaim for his novels.

To **garnish** is to 'decorate'. The word, which is verb or noun, is most often found in recipes, descriptions of dishes, etc. and refers to the small additions intended to make a meal look good and taste better.

GEEZER or GEYSER

Identical pronunciation sometimes causes confusion here.

Geezer is a slang term for a 'man' (preferably an old one).

A **geyser** is a 'hot spring, of water, mud or steam':

The volcano has been restless since 2001, with increased numbers of earthquakes, rising lake temperatures and geysers of boiling mud.

GOURMAND or GOURMET

There is widespread uncertainty over the distinction between a gourmand and a gourmet.

Being called a **gourmand** is not a compliment since it means a 'glutton', a greedy eater who doesn't mind what goes down as long as he/she gets enough of it.

A **gourmet** is a 'person with refined tastes in food and drink'. The word is also an adjective meaning 'refined', as here:

✓ The Chef wants to produce a gourmet meal in 30 minutes flat.

GRAND or GRANDIOSE

These two look alike but more separates them than unites them.

The difference between the adjectives is that **grand** should be applied to something which is authentically 'splendid', while **grandiose** suggests that what is described is somehow 'inflated' or 'false'.

A **grand** building is large and very imposing; a grand scheme is ambitious and conceived on a great scale. **Grandiose** ideas, by contrast, are hollow; they sound good but will never amount to anything.

GRILL or GRILLE

Both words describe metallic, perforated frames, and the frequent appearance of **grilled** (as in grilled meat) encourages the error of using the second where the first is intended.

A **grill** is a 'metal frame used in cooking':

She likes to cook on the gas grill.

A **grille** is a 'metal screen in front of a window or car radiator'.

(Grill is sometimes used in this sense of window lattice but grille should never be used for the cooking frame.)

GRISLY or GRIZZLY

Grisly is an adjective meaning 'terrible', 'gruesome'.

Grizzly means 'of a grey colour' (the same as 'grizzled'). In its noun use it stands for the grizzly bear (whose scientific name is Ursus), usually just referred to as the 'grizzly'. This is the spelling which is often confused with the first word.

H

HANGED or HUNG

These are the past tense forms of the verb to hang. There's a tendency to use hung for everything and everybody. Hanged should be used in one context, however.

In general, things should be **hung**. Pictures on walls, coats on racks, meat in the butcher's; **hung** can apply even to people when they are clinging on to something:

He hung from the window sill by his fingertips.

The single exception is in the context of capital punishment, when the individual is hanged. The wrong form of the word is often used:

✗ He was arrested immediately, found guilty of 'moral insanity' and hung [should be hanged].

HEROIN or HEROINE

That final 'e' makes all the difference, and the slip is easily made.

Heroin is the 'drug which is a morphine derivative', while **heroine** is the female equivalent of 'hero', a 'woman who shows heroic qualities' or the 'central woman character either in real life or in a story, film, etc.' Although there's a tendency now to use a single term to apply to both men and women in some artistic contexts — actor, poet — the hero/heroine distinction tends to be observed. It is even more important to preserve the heroin/heroine difference.

HISTORIC or HISTORICAL

Both of these terms derive from history but they carry fairly distinct meanings.

Historical is an adjective meaning 'relating to history', and attaching it to a noun says nothing about the significance of that noun. It's a 'neutral' word.

HOARD or HORDE

These two have the same sound and share overlapping ideas of mass and quantity.

A **hoard** is a 'hidden store' of something, usually valuable and put by for use in the future.

Horde describes a 'large number':
- ✓ There were hordes of people in the Central Market for the sales.

HUMILIATION or HUMILITY

The difference between these two words is considerable, but they look as though they might be related and confusion is possible.

Humiliation is 'shame' or 'treatment which hurts a person's self-respect'. The humiliation may be intended or unintended.

Humility is 'modesty', the 'capacity of being humble'. Fairly or not, it is sometimes presented as a slightly suspect quality, and associated with hypocrisy.

I

ILLEGIBLE or UNREADABLE

These two words both convey the idea of 'hard to read' but they have two different senses which are reflected in their definitions.

Illegible refers to the physical appearance of handwriting or print and means 'hard or impossible to read'. **Unreadable** can be used in this sense too although its principal application is to the quality of someone's writing, where it means 'so poor as to be not worth reading'.

IMPLY or INFER

This is a very familiar pair of confusables. People — or at least those who care — have long complained about the misuse of infer to mean imply.

Properly used, these verbs have a complementary quality. To **imply** something is to 'hint' or 'suggest' it without its being openly stated.

To **infer** is to 'draw conclusions from the evidence', and suggests skill at understanding hints and working out implications.

Infer is sometimes used as though it meant imply — as in the erroneous 'I don't like your tone of voice. What are you inferring?' This usage gets some dictionary support, but it is wrong by the standards of correct English.

INDIGNITY or INDIGNATION

An **indignity** is something that is inflicted or endured, an 'insult' or 'humiliation.'

Indignation is what the sufferer may feel about it afterwards, a sense of 'justified anger'. Indignation can be expressed on behalf of others and the unfair treatment they have received, as well as being felt for one's own sake.

INDUSTRIAL or INDUSTRIOUS

Both of these adjectives derive from 'industry' but they have acquired distinct meanings.

Industrial is used of objects, places, processes, etc. and means 'connected with the industry or the manufacture of goods':
- ✓ Industrial output remained high in the second quarter of the year.

Industrious is used only of individuals or groups of people and means 'diligent', 'hard-working'.

INFORMANT or INFORMER

Although both of these nouns describe a 'person who passes over information', they are used in different circumstances, one of which is more positive than the other.

An **informant** is a 'source' (who may be acting out of a sense of public duty to blow the whistle on wrongdoing, for example) and the stress is on the data he/she passes over.

The term **informer**, also describing a 'source', tends to be restricted to the person who names names, especially in police contexts.

INGENIOUS or INGENUOUS

Two words with a single-letter difference: They look as though they should be related but they are near-opposites.

Ingenious means 'clever', particularly in the context of finding solutions for problems or thinking up new methods.

Ingenuous means 'artless', 'simple' — usually too much so, as it's not innocence so much as gullibility that is suggested.:

✓ When he spoke about money it was with an ingenuous enthusiasm that offended no one.

(This adjective is more frequently found in its negative form: disingenuous.)

INHUMAN or INHUMANE

Both adjectives convey strong condemnation, and many people use them interchangeably. However, there is a distinction.

Inhuman, meaning 'brutal', 'barbarous', is the harsher of the two, and can describe an individual without any redeeming (human) features. More generally, it characterises people's behaviour towards each other, with the implication of being less than, not worthy of, a human being:

✓ We recall the inhuman treatment of concentration camp inmates.

Inhumane has the sense of 'cruel', 'lacking in qualities of kindness and sympathy', and is the opposite of 'humane'. It can be used about the way individuals or animals are treated.

INNOVATION or INVENTION

These two are closely connected but in no way mean the same thing.

An **innovation** is the 'introduction of something fresh' — not as radical as an invention, it's usually the development or refinement of an existing idea or system.

By contrast, an **invention** is a 'new device or discovery':

✓ Marconi is generally credited with the invention of wireless telegraphy.

Invention is also used in the sense of fiction — a 'deceit or lie'.

INNUENDO or INSINUATION

Both words describe something not openly stated but implied.

An **innuendo** is an 'indirect remark', very frequently one with sexual overtones — it's often the equivalent of the French phrase 'double entendre'.

An **insinuation** is more general, being any 'hint carrying an unpleasant suggestion'.

(To insinuate is to 'hint' but also to 'work (oneself) gradually into a place' — an organisation, a person's good books — by stealth.)

INOCULATE or VACCINATE

Two 'medical' terms that may appear to have distinct meanings but can, in fact, be used interchangeably in most contexts.

To **inoculate** is to 'protect against disease' by infecting someone with a mild form of that disease, so ensuring future immunity.

To **vaccinate** was originally to 'protect against smallpox by using the cowpox virus' (*vacca* is Latin for 'cow'). The word is now interchangeable with inoculate and applies to providing comparable protection from any disease. The only time inoculate should be preferred is in a metaphorical sense (e.g. if describing someone as 'inoculated against racism').

INSIDIOUS or INVIDIOUS

These two adjectives have nothing in common except for eight letters out of nine and their negative associations — it's enough to cause the occasional confusion.

Insidious points to a kind of slow-burning malice, and means 'cunning'. It can be applied to people but is more often used to describe words, attitudes, effects.

Invidious means 'causing bad feeling' or 'provoking envy'. Often qualifying 'position' or 'distinction', it should not be used as a synonym for 'difficult'.

INTENSE or INTENSIVE

There is some overlap between these two words and they can be found in the same context (intense/intensive questioning) but they also have distinct meanings.

Intense means 'strong' or 'characterised by extreme emotion'.

While intense can be used about people, **intensive** — meaning 'thorough', 'without relief or let-up' — characterises things like research and investigation.

INTERMENT or INTERNMENT

Interment is 'burial', almost always used literally.

Internment is 'confinement' (in a prison or camp). The word usually describes the pre-emptive treatment meted out to those regarded as potential troublemakers, spies, terrorists, etc. — that is, they are locked up as a 'precaution' and without the benefit of trial.

(The associated verbs are inter and intern. In the US and elsewhere, **intern** is also a noun meaning a 'trainee doctor in a hospital' or a 'person getting experience in any profession').

INVEIGH or INVEIGLE

These are two slightly unusual words which are sometimes confused, perhaps because of their similar spellings.

To **inveigh** (pronounced to rhyme with 'say' and always followed by 'against') is to 'attack strongly', usually in speech.

To **inveigle** (pronounced to rhyme with 'bagel') is to 'tempt' or 'coax'. The word carries the hint of something underhand.

ITS or IT'S

This is one of the commonest and most basic mistakes in written English. It's the apostrophe which causes the problem, of course.

It's is the contracted or shortened form of it is or it has:
- ✓ It's a warm day.
- ✓ It's been raining all day.

Its, without an apostrophe, is the possessive form of the pronoun it:
- ✓ The cat flicked its tail.

J

JUNCTION or JUNCTURE

Both words mean a 'joining or union' but occur in different contexts.

Junction tends to have a physical application, describing the point where roads or railway lines or electric wires meet. **Juncture** is a coming together in time rather than space, and suggests a 'critical point' in some process:

✓ At that juncture Dharmender and Hema Malini were able to announce their love to each other — but not to the world.

K

KNELL or KNOLL

A **knell** describes the 'sound of a tolling bell' — particularly at a funeral. In fact the word is almost always used figuratively and prefaced with 'death'.

The verb is also knell (past tense knelled).

A **knoll** is a 'small hill.

L

LAMA or LLAMA

It is surely the exotic source of these words — one from Tibetan, the other from Spanish via a Peruvian language - that sometimes causes confusion. There is nothing in them to hint at the meaning and so guide the spelling.

The **lama** with one 'l' is a 'Buddhist monk in Tibet'.

The **llama** with two 'l's is a 'four-legged beast of burden', the South American equivalent of the camel (in fact camels and llamas are related).

Don't confuse the man with the animal — for one thing, they come from opposite sides of the world.

LARVA or LAVA

A **larva** (plural larvae) is an 'animal, usually an insect, in the earliest stages of its development'.

Lava is 'molten rock from a volcano'.

LAST or LATTER

Last applies to anything coming at the end of a sequence (the last word, her last book) and means 'final', 'most recent'. **Latter,** whom properly used, should apply to the 'second of two items'.

LATITUDE or LONGITUDE

Latitude is the 'angular distance from the equator, measured to the north or south'. Latitude has the additional meanings of 'range' or 'freedom'. **Longitude** uses the meridian, any one of the great and imaginary circles running from pole to pole, with the meridian line through Greenwich taken as the starting point. Longitude is therefore the 'angular distance between a particular place and the Greenwich meridian, measured to the east and west'.

LAY or LIE

To **lay** is to 'put down' and is a transitive verb (i.e. one which is generally followed by an object):

Lay your sleeping head, my love…(first line of poem by W. H. Auden)

To **lie** is to 'be at rest on a horizontal surface' and is an intransitive verb (one which is not followed by a direct object):

✓ He told the dog to lie down at once.

Confusion mostly arises from the fact that the past tense of lie is lay:

✓ The dog lay down and went to sleep straightaway.

The past tense of lie is laid:

✓ They laid the picnic food out on the rug.

The past participle form (i.e. the one used after 'has' or 'had') is lain for lie:

✓ The farmhouse has lain empty for almost two years now.

LEACH or LEECH

There is a connection between the sense of these identically pronounced words, but also a distinction which should be observed.

To **leach** (only a verb) is to 'filter in or out'.

To **leech** is to 'suck the blood out of', to 'drain', from the noun leech, a 'blood-sucking worm'. (The word was once used in a slightly disparaging sense to mean a doctor — presumably because of the medical use of leeches in bloodletting rather than the fees which doctors charged.) Leech is frequently used to describe any parasitic individual or organization.

LESSEE or LESSOR

This pair of 'legalistic' terms is quite easy to confuse.

The **lessee** is the 'person to whom a lease is granted' (usually in property) while a **lessor** is the 'person who grants the lease'. A 'leaseholder' is the same as a lessee and a 'letter' (i.e. a person who lets) is the equivalent of lessor.

LIBEL or SLANDER

These two are often used interchangeably, although there is a difference between them not so much of meaning but of application.

Both nouns and verbs, **libel** and **slander** refer to a 'defamatory accusation' or mean to 'defame'. **Libel** is used about anything written or presented in permanent form, including material on the Internet.

Slander tends to be reserved for spoken comments.

LIBERTARIAN or LIBERTINE

These two words derive from 'liberty' so it's perhaps appropriate that they have moved off in different directions. One describes a political or ideological position while the other characterises a person who pursues sexual pleasure.

A **libertarian** is a 'person who believes in the maximum possible amount of freedom for himself/herself and others'. This usually entails freedom under the law but includes the right to pursue behaviour that might be self-destructive. The word is often associated with a particular branch of right-wing thinking.

A **libertine** is a 'person who leads a dissolute life, especially in sexual matters'. The term is a bit dated now and conjures up images of rakish.

LICENCE or LICENSE

This is a distinction that only emerges when the words are written.

The **'c/s'** difference applies to various words and is more fully discussed in the 'advice/advise' entry.

The noun form is **licence**:

TV licence; driver's licence; off-licence while the verb is license:

✓ 'Are you **licensed** to drive this vehicle, sir?'

LIGHTNING or LIGHTENING

Pronunciation tends to overlook the 'e' in the second word and spelling follows suit. The difference between the two is further blurred by their common root in 'light'.

Lightning, as an adjective, applies to anything which is 'moving very fast', and as a noun is the accompaniment of thunder, a 'burst of light in the sky':

✓ He was struck by lightning on the set.

This spelling is sometimes confused with **lightening,** meaning 'making lighter' (applied to reducing a burden or to changing a colour).

LIMP, LIMPID or LUCID

Limpid looks as though it must be connected to limp. It isn't. Its proper association is with lucid.

Limp means 'drooping', 'lacking firmness and authority'.

Limpid has nothing to do with the previous word but, if anything, is a near-opposite since it means 'very clear', 'transparent'. Frequently applied to music performances — often those at the piano, for some reason — it can also be used in more literal contexts.

Lucid has the same sense of 'very clear' and therefore 'easy to understand'. The context here is normally language, books and explanations.

LIVID or LURID

Both of these similar-sounding adjectives have connections with colour but are most widely used in other contexts.

Livid is 'dark', 'leaden':

✓ His cheeks are livid with bruises.

But it's most frequently used to mean 'extremely angry' (presumably because of the colour of an angry face).

Lurid has been used about a range of colour tones, from pale yellow to purple. In another sense it is also a favourite tabloid expression, generally applied now to news stories which have a 'sensational' quality.

LOATH or LOATHE

Both of these words convey an idea of hostility to something but they are different parts of speech, and used in different contexts.

Loath — with or, occasionally, without the middle a — is an adjective indicating reluctance, being 'unwilling'. It's a slightly literary and dated expression but still useful:

✓ I'd be loath to get involved in their quarrels.

Loathe is a verb meaning to 'regard with disgust':

✓ She loathed his flattering manner.

LOSE, LOOSE or LOOSEN

In their verb forms these words are occasionally confused, particularly the first two because of the doubling of the **'o'**. To **lose** or 'mislay' has one:

✓ The crowd on the streets in the old part of town made it easy to lose one's way.

To **loose** is to 'set free', 'cast off'.

To **loosen** is to 'make looser', to 'untighten', either literally or figuratively:

✓ A few drinks certainly loosened his tongue.

(The past tense forms are lost, loosed and loosened, respectively.)

LUSTFUL or LUSTY

Although both of these adjectives derive from lust, the meaning of one is essentially innocent.

Lustful is only connected to sex. It means full of 'lust', 'sensual', and hints at something passionate and perhaps forbidden:

✓ Boredom at work could be manifested by lustful dreams about a colleague

Even when **lusty** enters the sexual stakes the word has a jauntiness to it which is lacking in the altogether more biblical-sounding lustful.

LUXURIANT or LUXURIOUS

Both adjectives derive from luxury but have distinct meanings which shouldn't be confused.

Luxuriant describes anything which is 'produced in abundant quantities' or is 'lush' — its use is generally restricted to natural growth (hair, foliage, etc.).

Luxurious conveys notions 'of great comfort', expense and (sometimes) flashiness.

M

MACHO, MANLY or MANNISH

All of these terms relate to masculinity but they apply in quite different contexts.

To take the second word first, **manly** means 'brave', 'fitting for a man'.

It isn't used much now, perhaps because it has stiff-upper-lip, Victorian overtones. Masculine would be the modern equivalent.

Macho — from the Spanish word for 'male' — is a rough contemporary version but carries a suggestion of swaggering masculinity which the Victorians would certainly not have approved of.

Mannish can be applied to women who are considered insufficiently feminine — and for this reason it may sometimes be code for 'gay' or 'lesbian'.

MAJORITY or MOST OF

Both of these very ordinary expressions describe the greater part of something, and there is a tendency to use the first in all circumstances even when the second would be better English.

Majority is a noun meaning 'the greater number':

✓ The majority of the people in the poll favoured the death penalty.

Majority should not be used to mean 'the larger part' of something which cannot be split up into individual elements. When referring to a single unit, most of should be used, or another expression such as 'the greater part of':

I was on tenterhooks for the **most of** the film.

MALEVOLENT, MALICIOUS or MALIGNANT

Malevolent and **malicious** apply to individuals and their words or actions, in the sense of 'ill-disposed', 'wishing harm to'.

Malevolent is also used of animals. **Malicious** is perhaps less strong; a malicious remark (i.e. one that shows malice) may be nothing more than 'spiteful' while a malevolent one suggests something darker and more deep-rooted.

Malignant contains these meanings but, as indicated by its frequent application to cancerous tumours; it carries the more intense sense of 'causing harm or evil to'.

MANTEL or MANTLE

A switch-around of the last two letters produces a different word.

When the two are confused it's usually because the second, more familiar spelling is put in place of the first.

A **mantel** (usually mantelpiece) is the 'shelf above a fireplace'.

A **mantle** is a 'cloak or covering', but the word is very often applied metaphorically to mean 'status', 'authority'. In particular the handing over of a mantle suggests the symbolic moment when power changes hands.

MASTERFUL or MASTERLY

These two terms deriving from 'master' have an overlap of meaning but can carry different emphases.

The adjective **masterly** means 'highly skilled', 'brilliantly accomplished', and is most often used when a performance of sonic kind is being praised.

Masterful is often used to mean the same thing, but it carries overtones of 'bullying', of aggressive assertion, even if this is intended in a complimentary way.

MAY or MIGHT

There is a growing tendency to use **may** in all circumstances, even where might would be correct.

May is the present tense form:
- ✓ We think he may ring. (But we don't know yet whether he's going to.)

Might is the past tense:
- ✓ We thought he might ring. (Either he did ring or he didn't, but the sentence implies that we know one way or the other.)

MAY BE or MAYBE

As with other pairs such as 'all ready/already', the two-word version of may be is hardly distinguished in pronunciation from the single word. But when a mistake is made in writing the wrong meaning results.

May be is a combination of two verbs and is used when talking about a possibility:
- ✓ He hasn't answered but it may be that he didn't get my letter.

Maybe (one word) means 'perhaps':
- ✓ He hasn't answered but maybe he didn't get my letter

MEDIA or MEDIUM

Media, a collective term for 'means of communication such as television or newspapers', is the plural form of **medium.**

As a plural it should take the appropriate verb form:

✓ The media are influential in shaping people's opinions.

The tendency is to treat the word as a singular noun (an 'it' rather than a 'they').

MEDICAL or MEDICINAL

Both of these words are obviously connected to health and sickness but they have slightly different applications.

Medical means 'relating to the practice of medicine' (medical student, medical insurance) and, as a noun, describes a 'physical examination to check a person's health/fitness'.

The adjective **medicinal** means 'used in medicine' and so 'helping to cure'.

MERETRICIOUS or MERITORIOUS

These two quite similar sounding words have almost opposite - meanings, and the echo of 'merit' in the first word may mislead.

Meretricious has an interesting history since it derives from the Latin word meretrix meaning 'prostitute', and indeed its primary sense is 'relating to prostitution'. Never used in this sense now, it has come to mean 'flashy but without substance'.

Meritorious means 'worth praising':

✓ Being healthy is not meritorious in itself.

METAL or METTLE

The two are sometimes confused not only because of their identical pronunciation but because ideas of strength and toughness are common to both. Both words/spellings, in fact, have the same origin.

Metal describes 'any of the elementary substances such as gold or iron'. This spelling is sometimes used when mettle is meant. The confusion isn't surprising since both words are pronounced the same, and **mettle** carries the metallic-sounding idea of 'hardness', 'spirit'. When people are 'on their mettle' they are put in a situation in which they have to prove themselves.

METEOR or METEORITE

These two words refer to the same object but in a 'before and after' sense.

A **meteor** is a 'small object which turns to a fireball when it enters the earth's atmosphere'. Even small ones can do damage and the impact of anything larger could be terminal.

The term meteor can also apply to 'anything or anybody whose progress is bright but brief'.

More usual is the adjective **meteoric** to describe such a progress, often coupled with 'rise', as in 'her meteoric rise to the top of her profession'. **Meteors** do the reverse of going up, of course, although a belief stretching back as far as the ancient Greeks held that comets and other such objects actually emanated from the earth.)

A **meteorite** is what the meteor becomes when it has hit the earth: a 'lump of stone or metal':

✓ A meteorite from the Red Planet had been located in Antarctica.

METER or METRE

Both words are to do with measurement, and the slight difference in their endings is a recipe for confusion. In addition, the fact that US usage has only one form for both words (meter) makes things more tricky for those Brits who are influenced by American spelling.

A **meter** is a 'measuring instrument': parking meter; thermometer; milometer.

A **metre** is the 'basic unit of length in the metric system'(three metres in length, a kilometre further on). This is the spelling that is also used to describe poetic 'rhythm', the contrasting sounds between long and short or stressed and unstressed syllables in verse.

METHOD or METHODOLOGY

The longer, more impressive-sounding word is sometimes preferred to the shorter, more familiar one — but is it always necessary?

A **method** is a 'procedure' and a **methodology** is a 'system of procedures'. Methodology is a popular word in certain writing, usually of a rather bunged-up kind. Its use is legitimate when the writer really means a system of methods, rather than a random collection of them.

MILITATE or MITIGATE

These two verbs are often confused because of their similar look and sound but they have nothing in common.

To **militate,** generally followed by 'against', is to 'have weight', to 'operate'.

Mitigate has something of an opposite meaning — it is to 'lighten', to 'make less harsh'.

MISANTHROPIST or MISOGYNIST

Both of these terms are to do with dislike and hatred but one has a restricted sexual sense.

Misanthropy is a 'generalised distrust or hatred of everybody', men, women and children.

Misogyny is specifically 'hatred of women'.

These terms are often applied to attitudes displayed in film, music, etc. but they can be used about people in real life. Those who display such attitudes are the misanthropist (or misanthrope) and the misogynist.

MOMENTARY or MOMENTOUS

Both words derive from different senses of the same word, moment, but they can convey almost opposite meanings.

Anything which is **momentary** (pronounced with the stress on the first syllable) is very 'short-lived'.

Momentous (pronounced with the stress on the second syllable) means 'highly significant'.

MORAL or MORALE

These similar-looking words are sometimes confused — perhaps because of some subconscious association between behaving well (being moral) and feeling good (having high morale).

Moral as an adjective means 'connected to questions of right and wrong':

✓ 'We are not going to be moral guardians and stand in judgment'.

As a noun, moral is used in the singular only in the sense of 'lesson' (the moral of a story). In the plural, morals describe the 'principles or guiding beliefs' of a person or group, although it tends to have a sexual application only.

Morale characterises the 'spirit of an organised group' such as a body of soldiers or a football team.

✓ Their morale was sapped when shells began raining down on them and even the lighter shells pierced the ship's armour.

MUCOUS or MUCUS

One of these words is a noun while the other is the adjective derived from it, and it is easy to confuse the two spellings.

Mucus is the noun, describing the fluid secreted by a bodily membrane (e.g. the nose) in humans or animals.

Mucous is the adjective meaning 'mucus-like or slimy':

✓ Sulphuric acid is as dangerous as it sounds. Direct contact will burn the skin and play havoc with mucous membranes.

MUNDANE or WORLDLY

These two words are an interesting example of the way in which synonyms in English can, on the surface, share the same meaning while possessing different underlying senses.

Both terms mean 'of this world', but **mundane** carries the sense of 'everyday' (to the point of being boring).

Worldly is often used as part of compound words ('worldly-wise', 'other-worldly') but it also has a meaning of 'experienced in the ways of the world', 'sophisticated'.

N

NAKED or NUDE

This is quite a difficult distinction — and naturally an interesting one.

Naked is the more versatile word with its senses of 'without assistance' or 'lacking ornament' (naked effort, naked truth) as well as the basic meanings of 'bare', 'uncovered'. Naked is generally a less loaded or emotive word than **nude.**

Nude has associations with painting, photography and porn, and to that extent it could be equated with being 'intentionally naked' — often for artistic or sexual purposes.

The words aren't quite interchangeable.

NAVAL or NAVEL

Similar spelling and identical pronunciation sometimes produce a comic confusion over these two.

The adjective **naval** means 'relating to the navy'. The noun **navel** is defined by one dictionary as the 'depression in the centre of the abdomen' but is known to the rest of humanity as the 'belly/tummy- button'.

NEGLECTFUL, NEGLIGENT or NEGLIGIBLE

These words derive from neglect/negligence but have moved off in different directions.

Neglectful means 'inattentive', with the implication of failing to care for something or somebody:

✓ His busy life at work made him a rather neglectful father.

Negligent means 'careless', particularly in relation to

matters which are your responsibility and for which you may be held accountable.

Negligible means 'very slight or unimportant' (and therefore able to be neglected).

NICENESS or NICETY

'Nice' is a very old word with quite a range of meanings. Two of its spin-offs are niceness and nicety, but in terms of their meaning they are very distant cousins.

Niceness means the 'quality of being nice', 'agreeableness'. There's a blandness to the word or to what it describes, and it's often used with just a touch of criticism.

Nicety means 'precision' (as when something is judged to a nicety) or 'refinement' when it is usually found in the plural form, niceties.

O

OBJECTIVE or SUBJECTIVE

Both adjectives are to do with point of view. The difference between them is probably plain.

An **objective** approach is one which is 'unaffected by personal feelings', 'detached'.

Subjective means 'personal', 'taking one's feelings into account':

✓ But from a subjective viewpoint she resented the noise and pollution which the nearby road would cause.

Subjective is occasionally used in a critical way, as in 'You're taking a subjective point of view', with the unstated implication that only the speaker is being objective and giving an unbiased account.

OBSOLESCENT or OBSOLETE

These words, applied to equipment or machinery and sometimes to organisations, are stages in the same process and there is sometimes confusion over which comes 'first'.

Obsolescent means 'going out of date'.

Something which is **obsolete** is 'old', 'out of date' (and so useless).

OFFICIAL or OFFICIOUS

Both of these terms originally derive from the same Latin source but they have very different meanings. The second is sometimes used by mistake for the first, perhaps because people occasionally find that officials can also be officious.

As an adjective **official** describes a 'person or process that is properly authorised'.

The noun official is used of someone employed by a government department, as 'senior PMO officials'.

The adjective **officious**, by contrast, means 'interfering', with an overtone of fussiness:

✓ 'What are you two talking about?' he asked in his usual officious manner.

ORDINANCE or ORDNANCE

The one-letter difference between these two words, and the fact that pronunciation hardly distinguishes between them, can cause problems.

Ordinance - more common in the US than the UK - has the sense of a 'ruling' or 'decree' (especially in a local context):

✓ In the United States of America there are so-called weed ordinances banning lawns over a certain height.

Ordnance has the general sense of 'military equipment' but is almost always restricted in its application to 'artillery and ammunition'.

OUTSIDE or OUTSIDE OF

This is a stylistic distinction, with many people preferring to say or write outside of even though it's usually unnecessary.

There's not much justification for writing outside of when a simple outside would do. This is specially the case when **outside** refers to a place:

✓ They used to meet outside the building. (not outside of)

When referring to time, **outside of** is quite often used:

✓ They used to meet outside of office hours (but outside would do just as well)

When 'apart from' is meant, outside of is more acceptable:

✓ He had few interests outside of his work.

P

PANDA or PANDER

One of these words is a cuddly-looking animal, the other is a pimp. Take care over spelling.

The **panda** is the 'bear-like animal' from China (as well as a rather less well-known raccoon-like Himalayan creature).

It's not to be confused with a **pander** (sometimes spelled pandar) who is a 'pimp' or 'go-between' — the word has a slightly literary flavour but is always derogatory. As a verb, to pander is to 'gratify', to 'cater to the (low) taste of others':

✓ Maybe when they started price-cutting they felt they had to pander to their lower-brow recruits.

PEDAL or PEDDLE

Pedal as a noun describes a 'lever worked by the foot'; as a verb it is to 'operate such a lever':

✓ I pedalled fast to keep the other bikes in sight.

Pedaller is the associated noun (not very often seen). **Peddle**, a verb, is to 'sell small items'. When applied to any other kind of trade there is the suggestion of sleaziness or illegality: peddling lies, peddling drugs. Even when it's used in ordinary contexts it tends to disparage what is being 'sold'.

PEOPLE, PEOPLES or PERSONS

People means either an '(unspecified) number of individuals' or a 'whole national/racial/ethnic group' (the German people, the Maori people of New Zealand).

The plural **peoples** is restricted to this second sense and applies to the 'nations/racial groups of the world' — it's a slightly formal expression. The plural **persons** is formal and bureaucratic, and the only appropriate place for it is on notices: ('This bus seats 54 persons').

PERPETRATE or PERPETUATE

These quite similar-sounding words both contain the idea of 'carrying on/out'.

To **perpetrate** is to. 'carry out', to 'commit'. The noun that accompanies the verb is often 'crime' or 'outrage' (just as a perpetrator is frequently an 'offender', especially in the US where it may be shortened to the slang perp).

To **perpetuate** is to 'sustain', to 'make last':

✓ She avoids the moral high ground too, and never perpetuates the traditional literary myths of romantic love and happy endings.

PERQUISITE or PREREQUISITE

The similar beginnings and identical endings of these two words may occasionally cause confusion. In addition, both terms describe something which is conditional or dependent.

A **perquisite** is a 'benefit arising from employment'. The word is usually shortened to perk - as in 'perks of the job' - and would only be spelled out in full in fairly formal contexts:

✓ Among the perquisites of this position are frequent foreign travel and a generous entertainment allowance.

A **prerequisite** is a 'condition that must be met beforehand':

✓ Cost-effective production and a strong balance sheet are merely the prerequisites for survival.

PERSECUTE or PROSECUTE

The two verbs are sometimes confused, perhaps because they look similar and convey ideas of hostile action, but they have in fact nothing in common.

To **persecute** is to 'maintain a campaign of harassment' (particularly for political or religious reasons).

✓ First-time offenders may be warned by the police rather than **prosecuted**.

(Prosecute has the less familiar meaning of to 'pursue in order to accomplish'; in this sense a war or a political campaign can be prosecuted).

PERSON or PERSONA

The Latin word for 'person' is persona in expressions such as 'persona non grata'. But in English a person and his/her persona are not at all the same thing. What difference is produced by the addition of an 'a' to one of them?

A **person** is just a person, a 'human being' (and the word often carries a slightly dismissive note).

But a **persona** (plural personae) is something else — a 'public image', the 'face' assumed when dealing with the outside world' (the term originally comes from the field of psychology but is now widely used in general contexts.

PERSONAL or PERSONNEL

The spellings of these two words are sometimes confused, with the first being used in place of the second.

Personal is an adjective only, meaning 'relating to the individual', although it very often carries the additional meaning of 'private':

✓ He was unwilling to reveal his personal reasons for rejecting the job.

Personnel is a collective noun which describes the 'workforce' in a particular organisation. It's a bureaucratic word — rather impersonal in fact.

PERSPECTIVE, PROSPECTIVE or PROSPECTUS

This similar-sounding group contains ideas of views and visions.

A **perspective** is a 'point of view'. It's probably most widely used in the phrase 'put into perspective', which derives from the artistic technique of showing on a two-dimensional surface how objects seem smaller in the distance. So perspective becomes a way of assessing the relative importance - or lack of importance - of something, usually a problem.

The adjective **prospective** refers to the future and means 'expected', 'probable'.

A **prospectus** is the 'outline of some project which will materialise in the future' or it describes the advertising brochure issued by schools, colleges, etc. (To complicate the situation slightly, a prospect can also mean a view).

PERVERSE or PERVERTED

Although related, these two words have very different applications and should not be confused.

Perverse describes a person or an action that is 'contrary', obstinate', something hard to account for rationally.

Perverted has a sexual application almost exclusively, and characterises behaviour or attitudes that are 'deviant'.

Perverted still carries some weight and is generally applied to activities that are not merely off the beaten track but are also offensive. However, what is perverted to one man or woman may be another's standard liberated sexual behaviour.

As a verb **pervert** (stress on second syllable) is most frequently found in a legal context: to pervert the course of justice is to 'interfere with the proper process of the law' (by threats, bribes, etc.).

PHENOMENON or PHENOMENAL

Both of these words contain a kind of double meaning, and it may not always be clear which is meant.

At its simplest a **phenomenon** is no more than an 'observable event':

✓ Bluffing about books is a universal phenomenon.

Although the word easily shades into its associated sense of 'something extraordinary'. The adjective **phenomenal** is almost always used in this sense and signifies anything 'outstanding'.

Although phenomenal is often used casually for emphasis, particularly in its adverbial form — as in 'phenomenally boring' — it is preferable, at least in formal usage, to restrict the word to events which are truly 'remarkable'.

PIQUE or PIQUANCY

These related terms, both derived from French, characterise emotions or sensations that are linked by the idea of 'sharpness'.

Pique is 'bad feeling', 'wounded pride'.

(Pique is also a verb with the same meaning: to 'wound' or 'irritate').

Piquancy, a noun meaning 'sharpness', is often used to describe taste, particularly in its adjectival form (a piquant sauce), and generally has positive overtones. But the sensation may not always be so pleasant.

PITEOUS, PITIABLE, PITIFUL or PATHETIC

Too many closely related words all connected to the notion of 'pity'.

The first three adjectives mean 'arousing pity' or 'to be pitied', although with very slight differences in usage.

Piteous is not applied to individuals as such but to anything that moves us to feel pity.

Pitiable and **pitiful** can be applied to people and situations. Of the two pitiful is perhaps slightly stronger, suggesting someone who arouses pity through some visible means as well as by inner suffering, while **pitiable** is more to do with the latter:

✓ The searchers heard the piteous sounds of the trapped cat.

Both adjectives are also used to indicate mockery (a pitiful attempt).

Pathetic has a milder meaning of 'arousing sympathy', but usually carries an overtone, if not of contempt, then of superiority.

The colloquial use of **pathetic** to mean 'useless', or, more casually, as a term passing judgment on an unsatisfactory situation, can sometimes be a source of ambiguity.

POPULOUS, POPULAR or POPULIST

Three words connected to 'the people' and all deriving from the same source but with distinct meanings.

Populous indicates that an area is 'densely populated' (all cities are populous by definition), while **popular** means 'in favour', 'liked by many, or involving many people'.

Populist (noun and adjective) generally occurs in a political context and describes 'somebody who aims to appeal to the majority' (by offering to cut taxes).

PORE or POUR

The two verbs are sometimes confused, partly because they sound identical but also because both are frequently followed by 'over'.

To **pore** is to 'examine carefully.

To **pour** is to 'make flow'.

PORT or STARBOARD

Port is the left-hand side on ships (and on aircraft) while the **starboard** side is to the right, when facing forward.

PORTENTOUS or PRETENTIOUS

There's some overlap between these two weighty words but also a distinction.

Portentous comes from portent and so means 'ominous' or 'full of significance'. But it usually has the sense of 'self-important' too, and is rarely meant in a complimentary sense.

Pretentious also means 'self-important' shading into 'pompous'.

PRACTICAL or PRACTICABLE

A **practical** person or idea is a 'sensible and realistic' one. When applied to a plan, it suggests not only that it can be realised but also that it has merits:

✓ Within half an hour she came up with three practical ways of getting round the problem.

Practical carries the additional senses of 'good at making things' and 'down to earth' or 'actual' (as in practical experience as opposed to theoretical knowledge).

Practicable is not used about people, and indicates merely that something 'can be achieved', and not necessarily that it ought to be:

✓ Within the next few decades it is expected that manned flights to Mars will become practicable.

(The adverb practically carries the additional sense of 'almost', 'nearly': as in 'practically finished'. There is potential for ambiguity in a sentence such as 'the map was practically useless', which could mean either that the map was almost useless, or that it was useless for any practical purpose such as finding one's way - but could, for example, be hung on the wall as decoration.)

PRACTICE or PRACTISE

This is one of a group of word pairs which change by one letter between noun and verb (see also 'advice/advise', 'licence/license', etc.), and is probably the pair which is most often confused.

The **practice** spelled with a 'c' is the noun:

There are parallels between Indian and British business practices.

While the **practise** with an **'s'** is the verb:

✓ The band practised for most of the day.

PRAY or PREY

These two verbs are sometimes confused, with the first being used in error for the second. It's true that they sound the same but in this case that's not much of an excuse.

To **pray** is to 'beg for' or to 'ask during worship'.

To **prey** (on) is to 'kill for food' or to 'exploit' (with the suggestion of terrorizing).(The victim is the prey while the attacker is the predator).

PRECIPITATE or PRECIPITOUS

Precipitate, as an adjective, describes an action that is 'rushed', 'headlong'. As a verb it means to 'produce abruptly'.

Precipitous means 'steep':

✓ The railway cutting was extremely deep, and unusually precipitous.

However, precipitous is quite frequently used to describe an action which, in strict correctness, should be called precipitate.

PRESCRIBE or PROSCRIBE

A one-letter difference changes one word into its near opposite.

To **prescribe** is to 'direct', to 'lay down as a rule':

✓ The doctor prescribed plenty of rest and exercise.

To **proscribe** is to 'ban':

✓ The book has been proscribed by the Church.

(The nouns forms are, respectively, prescription and proscription. This second word is fairly rare).

PREVARICATE or PROCRASTINATE

To **prevaricate** is to 'avoid giving a straight answer'. Not as outright as lying, it is still evading the truth. To **procrastinate** is to put things off until later.

(The noun forms are **prevarication** and **procrastination**.)

PRINCIPAL or PRINCIPLE

The slight difference between the ends of these two words and overlapping definitions to do with guidance/leadership make confusion almost inevitable.

Principal is both noun and adjective, and means 'chief', 'most important':

✓ The principal things to remember, she was told, were to keep her speech short and relevant.

The most frequent application of the noun is to describe the 'head of a college or a school'. An additional noun meaning of **principal** is 'money on which interest is paid'.

Principle is a noun only, and means 'basic belief':

✓ There are principles here, they insist, and they should be examined before too much is given away.

PRISE or PRIZE

To **prise** is to 'force (open or away from)', using something as a lever — e.g. a crowbar or money.

Prized could be used in the example above, but prised is more usual in British English. (US spelling is prize only.)

A prize is a 'reward', and the verb means to 'place a high value on'.

PRODIGY or PROTEGE

A **prodigy** is a 'wonder'. Once used about signs and omens, it is now applied only to people. It's often associated with children who show very great talent in some field.

The word should not be confused with **protege** (more correctly spelled protégé), which describes a 'person who is under another's patronage or protection'.

PROGRAM or PROGRAMME

There is a tendency to use the increasingly familiar first spelling for all occasions in British English.

In the US, all **programs**, theatre, television, computer, are just that — programs.

British English has a spelling difference between the **programme** which you buy in the theatre, watch on TV etc., and the program which runs on a computer.

PROPHECY or PROPHESY

There's no problem with meaning here but sometimes a confusion over spelling.

Prophecy, meaning 'prediction' and pronounced to rhyme with 'see', is a noun:

✓ The sect's prophecy that the world was about to end was generally ignored.

To **prophesy,** to 'foretell', is a verb (pronounced to rhyme with 'sigh'). The verb doesn't carry quite the religious/messianic overtones of the noun, and can be used in the sense of 'forecast':

✓ The company prophesied continued growth for the rest of the year.

PSEUDONYM, PEN NAME or NOM DE PLUME

A **pseudonym** is a 'fictitious name', sometimes one assumed by writers but often by other people to ensure anonymity or protection.

A **nom de plume** is the same as a **pen name**; specifically a 'writer's assumed name' (as Mary Anne Evans took the name George Eliot at the beginning of her literary career). Oddly, nom de plume is not actually used in French — it joins a little list of phrases which you don't find in that country including 'son et lumière'.

Q

QUASH or SQUASH

The second word can almost always be used in place of the first, but the first has a more restricted application.

In a legal context, to **quash** is to 'make invalid' (convictions can be quashed or overturned). It has the more general sense of to 'crush out of existence' but not in a literal sense.

Apart from noun senses like 'fruit' and 'ball game', **squash** as a verb has the same meaning of to 'crush flat'. There's a more 'physical' quality to squash, which can be used both metaphorically and literally.

R

REBOUND or REDOUND

These verbs have essentially the same underlying meaning but they are not fully interchangeable.

To **rebound** is to 'spring back'. Even when not used literally, which it generally isn't, the word retains a kind of physical spring.

To **redound** is also to 'rebound' or 'be reflected back', but this rarer word is found in more dignified contexts: Balls don't redound, but words and behaviour do - to your or someone else's advantage, disadvantage, etc.:

✓ His policy always was to do what redounded to the credit of his wife.

RECOURSE, RESOURCE or RESORT

The three words are closely linked, and a dictionary will usually define them in terms of each other. However, there are small differences in their usage even if it's tricky to sort them out.

To have **recourse** to something means to go to it as a 'source of aid'.

Resort could be used as the verb in the sentence above ('We resorted to...'), giving the same meaning. This is more usual than the equivalent noun construction ('We had resort to...').

A **resource** is also a 'source of help', but the word doesn't normally convey the idea of turning to something in an emergency or a difficulty. More often it carries the related sense of a 'means' that one can draw on (a means of financial support, a way of filling one's time, etc.):

✓ Time didn't hang on his hands after retirement: he had plenty of resources.

Resource can also be a verb, usually in participle form: 'a properly resourced library'.

REGARDLESS or IRREGARDLESS

One of these words does not exist.

Regardless means 'without regard to', 'without taking into consideration'.

Irregardless does not — or at least should not — exist. But people occasionally use it in exactly the same sense as regardless. This non- word has probably come about through a confusion with 'irrespective' and/or a desire to create a more emphatic form of regardless.

REGRETFUL or REGRETTABLE

These two adjectives, with their connections to remorse and sadness, are sometimes confused in their applications.

Regretful relates only to people, and means 'capable of showing regret':

✓ Under cross-examination the defendant claimed to be regretful over what he had done.

Regrettable applies to incidents or situations (but not directly to people) which are 'causing regret':

✓ Then, in a regrettable turn of events, the company decided to close the factory.

The same distinction applies to the adverbs:

✓ Regretfully, she closed the front door for the last time.

✓ Regrettably, credit card debt is also the most widely available…

Regretful doesn't mean causing regret.

REIGN or REIN

Identical pronunciation and a shared sense of 'control' can cause confusion between these two.

To **reign** is to 'rule over'.

To **rein** is to 'control with reins' (used of a horse, young child, etc.) but it is most often used figuratively with 'in' to mean 'restrain':

✓ But the Pakistanis have done little so far to rein in the thousands of Taliban operating from Baluchistan.

This second word and sense are sometimes confused with the first.

RELIABLE or RELIANT

Reliable describes a person or system or object which can be relied on and carries the sense of 'dependable', 'trustworthy':

✓ It's a very reliable car — we haven't had a breakdown in five years.

Reliant (followed by 'on') applies to the people who do the relying and so means 'dependent'.

RESPECTIVE or IRRESPECTIVE

Respective means 'with respect to'. Respective and its adverbial form, respectively, are generally used when items in two lists are being matched up and indicate that the first item in list A is paired with the first in list B and so on.

Respectively has a function here as it makes clear which star takes which role. But the word is often used unnecessarily.

Irrespective means 'without regard to':

✓ Everyone else has to share out anything left over, irrespective of age and closeness to retirement.

RESTFUL, RESTIVE or RESTLESS

All three adjectives derive from rest, and the first and second are sometimes confused even though their meanings are opposed.

Restful means 'soothing', 'tranquil', and is applied, not to people, but to experiences that may have a calming effect, such as listening to a piece of music.

There is more than a shade of difference between the adjectives **restive** and **restless**. This latter word means simply 'unable to stay still'; unlike restive it does not imply that anyone is attempting to exercise control.

RING or WRING

Both of these words have a variety of meanings but there's one area in which the two come close - the idea of encircling with the hands— and this can lead to mistakes.

To **wring** has several meanings, including to 'twist' (as in, wring one's hands) and to 'extract' (wring out a confession from someone).

Ring, too, has a range of meanings from 'encircle' to 'call on the telephone'. One can ring a bird round the leg as a means of identification.

RISKY or RISQUE

These two words, one English, one French, amount to the same thing.

Risky means 'dangerous':

✓ The heavy snow and icy roads made for a risky drive home.

Risqué — generally with an acute accent on the 'e' — comes from the French *risquer*, which (surprise, surprise) translates as 'risk'. This word is only used in a sexual context. It describes a joke, picture, etc. which is 'suggestive'.

S

SANCTION or SANCTIONS

As a verb **to sanction** means to 'give permission'. It is a formal word.

Actually, the singular noun sanction can mean 'permission' or 'approval' — but, in practice, **sanctions** is almost exclusively used in the plural to describe the 'formal penalties' which follow from some infringement of laws or rules, as in economic sanctions that are being imposed.

SHALL or WILL

The difference between these two verb forms is generally sidestepped now, either by shortening both words to 'll (I'll, she'll), which buries the difference, or simply by using will across the board. But there is a difference...which is neatly illustrated by the old story of the two experts on English grammar who drowned. One threw himself into the river intending to commit suicide. To the people standing on the bank, he shouted, 'I **will** drown. And no one shall save me!' The other grammar expert fell in by accident. When he saw that no one was making a move to help him, what he called out was, 'I **shall** drown and no one will save me!' This does hint at the shall/will difference.

The distinction between the two is that, when all that is being expressed is simple futurity shall 'should' be used with the first person singular and plural (I/we) and will with the second and third persons (you/he/she/they):

✓ I/we shall see you tomorrow.
✓ You/he/she/they will be at the station at 6.30.

The shall/will link with particular pronouns is reversed when the sentence contains an element of compulsion or intention or determination: in short, anything that makes it more than a simple statement about the future. In these cases the first person (I/we) takes will while the others are followed by shall:

✓ 'I will do it, and there's no way you can stop me!'
✓ 'You shall go to the ball, Cinderella,' said the fairy godmother.

SHEAR or SHEER

Two words which are identically pronounced and whose spelling is easily confused. In addition, for the verb forms, there is a shared idea of movement, perhaps an abrupt one.

To **shear** is to 'clip' (as in sheep-shearing) and to 'cut'.

The adjective **sheer** means 'downright', 'absolute'.

As a verb to sheer means to 'swerve', 'turn from':

✓ He came prepared for a confrontation but sheered away from one at the last moment.

ASHOO-IN or SHOE-IN

Ashoo-in — the term was US slang originally and derives from a rigged horse race and is the 'inevitable winner of a race', a 'sure thing':

✓ Thank goodness the laws out there prevent foreigners from standing for President because Arnold Schwarzenegger, would be ashoo-in.

But a different spelling, **shoe-in,** is quite often seen although, strictly speaking, it is wrong. Interestingly, the mistake, which most likely comes from some association between fitting and shoehorns, may eventually push out the correct version.

SHOULD or WOULD

The difference between these two verb forms follows that for 'shall/will'.

Should can be used for the first person singular or plural:

✓ I/we should like to thank the speaker.

While **would** is appropriate for other pronouns:

✓ You/he/she/they would have arrived by now but for the traffic jam.

Should be used when the meaning of 'ought to' is intended:

✓ You really should try and see it.

SIMPLE or SIMPLISTIC

Simple has a range of meanings from the positive ('plain', 'unpretentious') to the negative ('gullible', 'silly'). But sometimes simple is just too simple to make the right impression, and so we reach for simplistic.

The two terms are not the same.

Simplistic means 'naive', 'oversimplified' and is almost always used in a critical sense. A simple plan may be a good one precisely because of its simplicity but a simplistic plan can never be good because it fails to take account of the complexities of a situation.

SITTING or SAT

Sat is increasingly used where better English would demand sitting.

This is an irritating mistake for anyone old enough to remember the way things used to be. Once, in a golden age of correctness, people were described as **sitting** round a table while a baby might be sat in its high chair. In other words, to be **sat** is to be put in your position (either by being directed to it or by being physically lifted onto a seat).

SOMETIME or SOME TIME

Pronunciation runs these two together, whatever the sense. On paper this is a fairly subtle distinction, but it is one that careful users of English will want to observe.

The single word **sometime** is an adverb, meaning 'at an unspecified or unknown point in time':

✓ 'Come up and see me sometime' was the actor' catch phrase. As an adjective sometime means 'former':

✓ She was a sometime magistrate and mayor of the town.

Some time (two words, adjective + noun) means 'for a period of time', usually quite a long period:

✓ For some time now we've been thinking of moving house. (Compare with We must move house sometime).

STATIONARY or STATIONERY

The endings of these words are pronounced the same, and it is easy to put the wrong one. A classic confusable.

Stationary (adjective only) means 'not moving':

The magician then asked the group to move the table with their minds. The table remained stationary, but the actor suggested it was moving.

Stationary (noun only) defines the paper, pens, etc. used in a workplace.

STIGMA or STIGMATA

These words change meaning between the singular and the plural.

A **stigma** is a 'mark of shame or disgrace', although the word is generally used less intensely.

The plural version of the word, **stigmata**, is only found in a religious context since it refers to 'the five wounds which Christ received on the cross' (from nails and spear).

The verb to **stigmatise** - meaning to 'brand with shame' arid so to 'condemn' — is popular in our culture just now.

STRAIGHT or STRAIT

Identical pronunciation and a blurring of meanings between 'narrow' and 'unbending' sometimes cause these two to be confused.

The adjective **straight** means 'direct', 'without a curve' and so by extension, honest'. The noun use is mostly found in a racing context and in the singular.

Another principal noun (and adjectival) use is a slang or informal one to mean 'heterosexual'.

Strait is an out-of-date adjective meaning 'narrow', 'confining', and is now used only as part of a couple of longer words, straitjacket and straitlaced.

As a noun, almost always in the plural, strait(s) describes 'a narrow stretch of water between two seas' or has the sense of 'difficult circumstances', often with 'dire' in front of it:

✓ After the house sale fell through they found themselves in dire financial straits.

STRATEGY or TACTICS

Strategy has long since moved from its origins as a word of war (where it means 'generalship', 'campaign planning') and now encompasses any 'large-scale and long-term planning'. In the 1990s especially it broadened out to become a favourite term in education and the 'soft' sciences, producing expressions such as 'classroom strategies', 'learning strategies', etc.

Tactics — very often used in the plural — underpin strategy, that is, they are the 'means to reach a goal', the detailed manoeuvres that enable a strategic plan to be realized.

SUGGESTIBLE or SUGGESTIVE

Two terms connected to suggestion but with widely different uses. Both are slightly pejorative.

Suggestible means 'open to suggestion' and so 'gullible' or 'easily influenced'.

But **suggestive** generally defines comments which contain a double meaning or have a sexual undertone:

✓ The writer was a diffident, ceremonious man unlikely to risk suggestive remarks to his upright publisher.

T

TAIL or TALE

A **tail** is the 'posterior extremity of an animal'. It has a slang application to buttocks and/or genitals. And in cricket, tail describes the players who are put on to bat at the end.

A **tale** is a 'story', often one which is spoken rather than written down and sometimes with overtones of childhood (as in The 'Tale of Peter Rabbit). It can be true or fictitious or just plain malicious (in the sense of 'telling tales').

TEMERITY or TIMIDITY

These two nouns are opposites.

Temerity means 'daring', with the suggestion of rashness. It is more usually applied to, say, challenges to authority than cases of physical daring. **Timidity** points to an opposite attitude: 'lack of nerve', a shyness that makes its possessor unassertive:

✓ Timidity made him reluctant to speak out even when his own interests were being threatened.

THEIR, THERE or THEY'RE

Uncertainty over the spelling of these three words, particularly the first two, is very common.

Their is the possessive form of the pronoun 'they' — indicating something that belongs to 'them':

✓ They wanted the cash to begin a business .

There is an adverb of place ('over there') or is used to start a sentence or introduce certain verbs (especially 'to be'):

✓ 'There were moments when we were in real trouble.'

They're is the short form of 'they are'.

THROES or THROWS

Throes (always found in the plural and nearly always preceded by 'in the') are 'spasms' or 'pangs of pain' — they were originally birth pangs. The word retains something of this old meaning, since it applies to painful processes which are not yet complete:

✓ The country is in the throes of a bitter power struggle between reformers and the ruling conservative leaders.

Throes shouldn't be confused with **throws,** plural of the noun throw ('casting', 'act of throwing', 'a loose covering').

TITILLATE or TITIVATE

To **titillate** is to 'tickle', to 'mildly excite', almost always with a sexual application.

The similarity in sound between titillate and **titivate** — or an artificial emphasis on the first syllable of the second word — may suggest a sexual meaning here too, but in fact titivate is to 'tidy', to 'make smarter':

✓ I want them to think well of me and the garden. So I have been going round tidying and titivating.

TORPID or TORRID

Torpid means 'sluggish':

✓ The hot weather made the animals torpid.

Torrid means 'scorching', 'parched':

✓ The torrid climate meant we couldn't go out during the day.

(The most usual application of torrid is in its associated sense of 'hot with passion'. Others include 'sensual', 'explicit', 'frank', and the old favourite 'steamy'.)

TORTUOUS or TORTUROUS

Both of these words suggest something unpleasant or worse, and pronunciation sometimes blurs them into one by overlooking the second 'r' in torturous.

Tortuous means 'twisting' or 'highly complicated':

✓ We almost got lost on the tortuous mountain path.

Torturous derives from torture, and means 'causing severe physical or mental pain':

✓ I spent a torturous hour in the traffic jam.

TRAVELLER or TOURIST

Two words which mean almost the same thing but which carry different overtones.

A **traveller** (US traveler) is 'one who travels' (and the term also has the specialised sense of 'travelling salesman or saleswoman'). There's a sense of purpose to the word, as in 'business traveller', and often of adventure. Bookshops and newspapers have travel, not tourist, sections.

A **tourist** is 'one who travels for pleasure', a 'sightseer'. There's sometimes a touch of criticism in the word, particularly in a phrase such as 'health tourist', which implies travelling with the sole purpose of taking advantage of some facility or amenity of a country.

TRIUMPHANT, TRIUMPHAL or TRIUMPHALIST

Three words relating to victory, one in a positive sense, one neutral and one critical. Care is required to tell them apart.

Triumphant means 'rejoicing in victory', and generally applies to individuals, teams, etc. and their words and reactions after they've won:

The team was triumphant after their fifth victory in a row.

Triumphal describes rather the process of 'commemorating a victory'. So an arch or a column - or a march - could be triumphal.

Widely used now is the adjective **triumphalist**, suggesting 'gloating in victory', and the noun **triumphalism** — these words carry a critical note because they convey a cocky revelling in success.

TROOPER or TROUPER

A **trooper** is a 'private soldier' (and in the US also a state policeman).

A **trouper** is 'someone who plays in a troupe of actors or other performers', usually admired for his/her longevity and resilience.

TRUSTEE or TRUSTY

Both of these nouns are related to trust but you would not be thanked for confusing them.

A **trustee** - pronounced to sound the double 'ee' - is a 'person who is entrusted with managing property or an organisation' (often for charitable purposes).

A **trusty** is a 'person in jail who has earned special privileges' (usually through good behaviour), although I am told that the word has not been used for many years. As an adjective, trusty means 'reliable', although for some reason it's hard to imagine the word being used without a touch of irony.

U

UNDERLIE or UNDERLAY

The 'lie/lay' distinction is a recipe for disaster (see relevant entry for an attempt at explanation), and this related pair is no exception.

To **underlie** is to 'lie beneath'. The present participle/adjectival form is underlying and the past tense form is underlay; the word is normally applied to abstracts such as ideas and principles.

To **underlay** is to 'lay under' — i.e. to 'place something underneath something else'. The past tense form is underpaid. This verb is rarely found, and underlay is more often used in its noun sense to describe the 'felt, rubber, etc. placed beneath a carpet'.

USE or UTILISE

This is a bit like the 'begin/commence' distinction, with people choosing the longer word because it looks more impressive.

Utilise suggests an active putting to use of whatever one can find:

✓ Robinson Crusoe utilised the resources of his desert island.

Use is a plainer term:

✓ She used her knowledge of languages to get along with people.

Utilise is often used because **use** doesn't sound sufficiently weighty.

But the shorter word is normally good enough.

V

VALUABLE or INVALUABLE

The 'in-' prefix to invaluable sometimes causes people to assume it is the negative form of valuable (probably by analogy with 'incorrect', 'indecisive', etc.).

The opposite of **valuable** ('having worth') is 'valueless' or 'worthless'. People may occasionally use **invaluable** in this second sense, but its correct meaning is 'not capable of being valued' or 'beyond price' — and therefore very valuable indeed. It tends not to be applied to objects.

VENAL, VENIAL or VERNAL

The first two words are quite similar in sound and both have overtones of wrongdoing.

Venal means 'open to being bribed' and so 'corrupt'.

Venial, usually used with 'sin' or 'offence', means 'forgivable'.

Neither word should be confused with **vernal**, meaning 'connected to spring'. Once a poetic term, this word is perhaps not much used now except in 'vernal equinox', the date in late March when the night and day are of equal length.

W

WAIVE, WAVE, WAVER or WAIVER

A group of words which look alike and are quite often confused. The gesture of waving possibly links up to the underlying idea behind waive and waiver.

To **waive** is to 'forgo', to 'hold back from claiming an entitlement'.

A **waiver** (noun only) is the 'act of waiving' or, more usually, a 'document which shows this', that is, it indicates that the possessor is exempt from some fee or charge.

Wave has a variety of meanings including to 'signal' and to 'move in an undulating way' and cannot be used in the sense of waive.

WASTE or WASTAGE

These two words relate to something unused or unneeded but there is a wide difference between them.

As a noun or verb **waste** characterises activities which are extravagant or useless (a waste of money, to waste time) while the adjective waste describes anything which is 'unused' or 'rejected' (waste ground, waste paper).

Wastage refers to 'inevitable loss through use or decay'. Now we have come up with the expression 'natural wastage' to describe the process whereby companies can reduce their workforce through retirement, death on the job, etc. rather than through compulsory redundancy. It's a wonderfully sterile phrase.

WEATHER, WHETHER or WETHER

These three words, two of them part of basic vocabulary are quite often mixed up, with confusion over when or whether to include two 'h's.

Weather is 'atmosphere', sun, rain, etc.

Whether is a conjunction introducing the first of one or more alternatives (whether…or).

A **wether** is a 'castrated ram'.

A **bell-wether** — which can be male or female — is the leading sheep in a flock, followed by the others because it has a bell hung round its neck.

WHISKY or WHISKEY

Two drinks with a certain amount in common, and a one-letter difference.

The standard English spelling of **whisky** (i.e. the stuff distilled in Scotland) doesn't have an 'e'.

But the **whiskey** which is produced in Ireland or America takes the 'e' (and this is the standard US spelling).

WHO or WHICH

When to use **which** as opposed to **who**?

Who is used for individuals:

✓ The man who broke the bank at Delhi…

Which tends to be for events, objects, etc.:

✓ There was a historic battle which took place on this spot.

WHO'S or WHOSE

Two 'grammar' words, **who's** and **whose**, with identical pronunciation and very similar spelling.

Who's is the contracted form of who is. **Whose** is the possessive form of who. Although the words sound the same they have completely different functions.

WILE, WHILE or WHILST

As a noun **wile** describes a 'trick', but there's often something pleasant or seductive about it.

To **wile**, a rare verb, also means to 'trick' or 'beguile'.

Wile has nothing to do with **while** - or **whilst**. As conjunctions these two words mean exactly the same thing ('during'), but **whilst** has a slightly fussy, pursed-lips quality to it.

WINNING or WINSOME

Two words that both sound positive, even synonymous unfortunately one can be loaded, even critical.

Winning, apart from its sense of victorious (the winning team), can mean 'engaging' or 'persuasive': a **winning** smile, a winning speech.

Winsome has absolutely nothing to do with 'win'. Although it can carry the sense of 'attractive', it is almost always used in contexts which suggest something rather 'cute and calculated'.

WREAK, WRECK or REEK

Wreak and **wreck** are often mixed up because their meanings are close, although they are pronounced differently (wreak with a long '*ea*' sound, as in 'week'). To **wreak** is to 'bring about harm', to 'inflict vengeance':

✓ Wherever the storm went, it wreaked a trail of havoc.

To **wreck,** on the other hand, is to 'destroy', or to 'spoil something so completely as to put it out of action'.

To **reek** is to 'give off smoke or fumes' and generally applies to unpleasant smells or, metaphorically, to anything unattractive or corrupt. This term is also confused with wreak despite having a quite different meaning because the two words are pronounced the same. The right use is:

✓ After all, no one will want to buy into a brand that reeks of doom and closure.

Y

YIN or YANG

Yin and **yang** are Chinese terms describing the complementary (but opposed) principles which underlie religion, medicine and so on.

Yang is the 'active male principle', light and warm, while **yin** is the colder and more passive 'feminine principle', each necessary to the other, held in a state of balance and tension, etc. As with various imports from Chinese culture, such as fengshui, originally serious ideas have been largely reduced to advertising props or lifestyle adornments for the west.

YOKE or YOLK

The noun **yoke** is 'anything that joins items/people/animals together', with a verb meaning of 'link'. In a concrete sense the yoke is a 'frame that fits round the neck' (of oxen, for example) and, metaphorically, it can also stand as a 'symbol of oppression or slavery'.

Yolk is the 'yellow part of an egg'.

YOUNG or YOUTHFUL

Both words mean roughly the same, but using **youthful**, despite its being a positive term, could cause mild offence in the wrong context.

Young tends to be neutrally descriptive but youthful carries overtones of 'fresh and vigorous'. It's quite often used not about the young (who are naturally youthful) but about older people who've retained - or clung onto — the habits, attitudes, etc. of earlier days. If you describe someone as having a youthful appearance the implication is that they look younger than they are, often surprisingly so. But in other contexts the word may not always be complimentary.

YOUR or YOU'RE

Your is the possessive form of the pronoun 'you':

✓ Don't forget your toothbrush.

You're is the shortened form of 'you are':

✓ You're not going to believe this!

Reversing these (you're toothbrush/your not going to) is a bad mistake.

As with the confusions over 'its/it's' and 'whose/who's', the way to check which one is correct is to experiment with the full-length version, in this case 'you are'. If it makes sense then 'you're' is correct, if you want to abbreviate the expression. If it does not make sense, then the word you intended to write is 'your'.

Z

ZENITH or NADIR

The **zenith** is the 'position in the sky directly over the observer's head', and so comes to mean 'high point', 'most flourishing period'.

The **nadir** is the 'direct opposite of the zenith', and if taken literally would apply to the position under the observer's feet, but it is rarely used in this celestial or astronomical sense and means rather the 'lowest point', the 'worst period'.